the rum cookbook

books by the same author

the rum cookbook

Alex D Hawkes

Drake Publishers Inc   New York

acknowledgments

I would like to express sincere thanks to the following persons and establishments in Jamaica, for their assistance in various ways during the preparation of this book.

J. Wray and Nephew Limited, particularly Mr Richard D'Costa
Miss Maria LaYacona, photographer
Mr Vincent Campbell, for his continuing patience and attention
Leonard DeCordova Limited, particularly Mrs Keith Ellis
Devon House, particularly Miss Dora Hanna
Golden Dragon Restaurant, Mr and Mrs Winston Lee
Mr Braddy Hale, of Bryden and Evelyn Company Limited
Honey Bun of Spanish Court, Mr Robert Hamilton and colleagues
Magic Kitchen, particularly Mr Wolfgang Höhn and Mr George Hannam
Mr and Mrs Arthur D. Myers, of Edwin Charley (Jamaica) Limited
The Sheraton-Kingston Hotel, particularly the general manager, Mr Russell Schmidt, the resident manager, Mr Robert Purrington, and the exceptional bartender, Mr Vivian Adams

The publishers wish to thank J. Wray and Nephew Limited without whose assistance the publication of this book would not have been possible

Hawkes, Alex D.   1927 –
   the rum cookbook
   1. Cookery (Rum)   2. Alcoholic beverages
1. Title.
TX726.H37   641.6'2   73–3097
ISBN 0 87749 446 0

Publlshed in 1973 by
Drake Publishers Inc
381 Park Avenue South
New York, N.Y. 10016

contents

colour plates

This book is dedicated, with fond affection, to Mr and Mrs Morris Cargill of 'Charlottenburgh,' Highgate, St Mary, who first introduced me to the continuing delight of Jamaica rums on their home grounds.

an introduction to jamaica rums

The drinkable spirits of the world are considerable in number and diverse in degree of popularity. In terms of world-wide consumption, four types stand out above all others, rum, whisky, gin and brandy. Rum, particularly the rum produced in Jamaica, is increasing in popularity all over the world.

The history of rum is a rather lengthy one, but there are some rather conspicuous gaps in the story. For instance, the precise origin of the very name rum itself is relatively uncertain. The word itself first appeared in recorded literature during the early or middle seventeenth century and was long thought to be a possible derivative of English slang, meaning 'something very good or tasty'. Oddly enough, rum as a word, in its vernacular sense, later came to signify poor, bad or inferior, the exact opposite of tasty.

Then there is the version which is more logical. On Christopher Columbus's 3rd voyage to the New World, he planted sugar cane in Hispaniola. The colonists soon found that a pleasing and intoxicating drink could be made by distilling fermented meleza, the sticky rich brown residue from the cane, which we call molasses. At first this powerful drink was called aguardiente de caña, or literally liquor from cane. Later, it became known as saccharum, this being the contemporarily accepted botanical genus name for sugar cane. British sailors plying the Spanish Main, soon became very well acquainted with the Caribbean drink and shortened the saccharum to rum.

Rum was, for a very long period, considered solely the drink of sailors and persons of low status. With the advent of cocktails in the 1920's, however, the drink became socially acceptable. This was really the starting point for the contemporary world-wide importance of our superlative Jamaican Rums.

Today, our rums in all of their variety, are drunk in many ways. They can be taken on-the-rocks, all the way to ornate and frequently highly potent creations in large specially designed containers, adorned with everything from fresh orchid flowers to bamboo sticks or swizzles of peeled sugar cane. Rum, as I will point out in the pages of this book, is also increasingly popular as a delicious and interesting ingredient in gourmet cookery.

Rum is the spirit obtained by distilling the fermented products of the sugar cane, Saccharum officinale, which is technically a member of the Grass Family. Wherever cane is grown, rum is usually made. Rum was first produced on a commercial basis in Jamaica and today Jamaica is one of the most important rum producing countries.

Jamaica rums have an enviable reputation with connoisseurs throughout the world today. Its production is stringently supervised by the Government. The process is a proportionately lengthy and time-honoured one, with bonded ageing from four to twenty years and the results are of prime calibre. There are many different name brands of Jamaica rums available, both on the international and local markets. These vary from light, white and clear, to dark and syrupy, to the highly flavoured and on to the few of liqueur quality.

Rum is produced in many countries. The U.S.A. for example, is the world's largest producer in terms of volume with Puerto Rico in second position. Mostly, however, these rums are scarcely aged at all and as a result have a rather raw taste in comparison to the fine Jamaica rums. Cuba used to be a big distiller of rum and various other of the Caribbean islands, Hispaniola, Barbados, Trinidad and Martinique still contribute supplies to the world market. Demerara rum from Guyana is well known and Mexico has several distilleries. Brazil and Bolivia both produce several kinds and rums also originate from South Africa, the Malagasy Republic, Australia, and Indonesia. Russia produces small amounts of very high ester rum, from fields principally near historic Tashkent, in Turkestan.

The distillation of rum utilises molasses, the

most important by-product of sugar production. This might, if it were not for the rum producers in Jamaica, be wasted, since we do not frequently use molasses for human consumption. It is often thought of as only an additive to fodder for cattle.

In past years, Jamaica boasted of some 38 rum distilleries. The number has now fallen to about 9 on the sugar estates. The rum producing phase of these estates provides a regular profit each year.

The distillation process for rum was introduced into Jamaica about 1655, with the British conquest of the island. A famous old distillery stood on the site of the present University of the West Indies at Mona, where some prime rum was produced. This establishment ceased operations in 1907 and today the Mona rum is exceedingly rare and expensive, though coveted by connoisseurs both here and abroad.

The British Navy has, until recently, given each man a daily rum ration, this primarily of imported Jamaica Rum. The ration, incidentally, was a large 5 oz per man of rum at just five under proof!

Many people drink their Jamaica rums over ice these days, so that the full body of the drink can be savoured. The various primarily local concoctions such as rum and grape juice, or the incredible rum and chocolate milk are short-lived and today most rum is drunk either neat or with mixes of special liquids or water. Numbers of Jamaicans and enterprising imbibers abroad, keep their prime rum bottle in the refrigerator knowing that this permits full appreciation to the palate.

Rum sales are at an all time high today, in all parts of the world. A very considerable percentage of these sales fall to the superlative and varied types produced here in Jamaica.

visit to a jamaica rum distillery

I think that every resident of, and visitor to Jamaica should pay a visit to one of our unique rum distilleries. The production of rum for the international market is big business and all who relish the remarkable Jamaican rums will appreciate these special spirits more after seeing exactly how they are made.

Fortunately, the public can easily visit the fascinating plant at J. Wray & Nephew Ltd.'s, Appleton Estate, in the parish of St. Elizabeth, and I think a resumé of my trip there will typify the activities of the majority of our distilleries. Advance arrangements should be made, unless you join one of the frequent scheduled tours which are offered from Kingston and Montego Bay. From Montego Bay it is possible to take the popular Governor's Coach Tour, a special scenic train tour with a stop at Appleton. From Kingston, visitors can take the train, alighting at Appleton, or else arrive by bus, taxi or car.

I drove up from Kingston for the day. It is a wonderful trip and takes you through many attractive parts of the Jamaican countryside and the Appleton Estate brings you into the margins of the fabled and virtually unexplored Cockpit Country. The scenery around Appleton is thrilling to everyone. When I was there many of the splendid huge tropical trees, such as Royal Poinciana and African Tulip Tree were in full blossom and made the district even more photogenic than usual.

My colleague and chauffeur, Mr Vincent Campbell, and I were met by Mr Norman Rowe, who after a most cordial welcome, introduced us to Mr Michael Delevante, the supervisor of the distilleries. He showed us through all parts of the extensive establishment and answered our queries. Mr Delevante is the author of an informative illustrated pamphlet entitled 'The Appleton Story' available at the distillery and has given me permission to quote from its pages.

The process of manufacturing Jamaica rum is an involved one, requiring time and patience. It involves three separate stages, fermentation, distillation and ageing. As I have noted earlier, the rum produced by Jamaican methods is unique in the time taken and in the close attention to detail. It requires, in many instances, a period of several years and many people agree that the end product is superior to all other varieties of rum made anywhere else in the world today.

My host, Mr Delevante, conducted Mr Campbell and I to two small, hot, 'no entry' rooms where we were shown the culturing of the particular species of yeast cells which are needed for the process. This culturing is done under sterile controlled conditions in test tubes and chemical flasks. It struck me as rather odd that the tiny grey smears on the agar seaweed jelly in the tubes were largely responsible for the rum that I have at home. The yeast cells are added to tanks containing a mixture of molasses and water and reproduce rapidly and in large numbers.

From these culture tanks, the mixture is introduced into larger vats filled again with molasses and water solution, where fermentation occurs. Basically, the dissolved sugar in the molasses is absorbed into the wall of each microscopic yeast cell, where it is converted into alcohol and carbon dioxide gas. Peering into the giant containers through glass view pieces reminded us very much of some eerie 'witches brew'! Eventually, after approximately 33 hours, the yeast cells die, because all of the sugar has been utilised. These cells settle to the bottom of the vat and are eventually drained off and discarded. At this stage the bubbles of carbon dioxide no longer come to the surface and a liquid of 7 per cent alcohol is obtained. The various mixtures are pumped from one vat to another, until all possible alcohol is drawn from the fermenting molasses and water mixture.

Two kinds of distilling stills are used in Jamaica, the pot still and the continuous still. The pot stills are large, bulky structures and were the original method for rum distillation. Many rum manufacturers have discarded these pot stills in favour of the more modern and more efficient continuous stills. At Appleton, however, they still use some pot stills for certain types of rum.

The pot still gives a heavily flavoured rum, one containing about 85 per cent alcohol and 15 per cent water. The continuous still contains only about 5 per cent water the remainder being alcohol. At the Appleton Estate, two sets of the continuous stills produce rum, the third produces alcohol. All of this process is controlled by a most impressive array of gauges and control levers and dials, which are constantly supervised.

When distilled, rum is colourless. After distillation, Jamaica rum goes through maturation, the ageing period being from four to twenty years in 40-gallon barrels made of oak wood. During this ageing, which Jamaican distillers consider essential to the quality of their product, the wood from the casks imparts both a characteristic and distinctive flavour and colour to the spirits. A few gallons from each barrel are lost by evaporation.

We were escorted into the inner part of the 'ageing warehouse', which is an immense structure and by nature very cool even on the hottest of days. It is a very impressive sight to see the endless tiers of barrels, all containing various types of maturing Jamaica rum in different stages of development. Each is marked with an intriguing series of symbols designating the contents, pertinent dates and other details.

The rum remains in the distillery warehouse, under Jamaican Government bond until it is required by the bottlers in Kingston. It is then sent in large, specially designed tanker trucks. At the bottlers, rums from both the pot still process and the continuous still process are blended, reduced with water to the desirable strength, and bottled by machines.

I asked during my tour of the distillery at the Appleton Estate, just what the word 'proof' as applied to rum and other spirits signified. Mr Delevante explained it by saying that it was an arbitrary standard, established on a basis of 100 proof. The liquid under consideration for proofing burns but does not ignite nor explode when it contains 57 per cent of alcohol and 43 per cent of water. The American proof system is different, being based on a ratio of 50 per cent alcohol to 50 per cent water, hence labels of rums and other spirits can be misleading and confusing. The American system is exactly double that of the French one, still utilised in certain rum producing areas, including the French islands of the Caribbean.

At Appleton, 750,000 proof gallons are produced each year. Some considerable proportion of the alcohol derived from the continuous stills goes into the manufacture of vodka and gin. Famous liqueurs are also made from the same base and have many flavourings and colourings added. These come from the far corners of the world ranging from cinnamon bark and orris root to juniper berries.

Much of the rum produced in Jamaica is drunk here. But exports are increasing to many parts of the world and the future of the many fine brands of Jamaican rum is certainly well assured. Jamaican rums are unique and prized and appreciated as such by connoisseurs everywhere.

jamaica rum drinks

doctor bird cocktail
serves 1

The national bird of Jamaica is the Streamertail Humming Bird and is one of the most extraordinary creatures to be seen anywhere. It is known locally as the Doctor Bird and though it is very common here, it is found only in Jamaica. The Doctor Birds are noisy and argumentative and drive off any possible intruder from their especial territory.

1 jigger* light Jamaica rum
1 teaspoon honey, logwood if available
1 teaspoon cream
dash or two grenadine syrup
cracked ice
fresh flower for garnish

Combine all ingredients, shake thoroughly and strain into a chilled champagne glass. Garnish with a rinsed bougainvillea or other fresh flower.

bacardi cocktail
serves 1 or 2

A Bacardi is a classic rum cocktail, originating in Cuba, and named after a famous old rum family there. White or light Jamaica rums make an interesting substitute for the Cuban variety, with subtly distinctive results.

2 jiggers white or light Jamaica rum
juice of ½ ripe lime
2 dashes grenadine syrup
cracked ice

Combine all ingredients, shake until frothy, and serve in cocktail glass, without garnish.

* 1 jigger = 1½ ozs

daiquiri   serves 1

The Daiquiri is one of the most famous of all rum cocktails and, as would be expected, everyone makes it a little differently. Here is the classic recipe which, please note, uses powdered sugar rather than simple sugar syrup.

1 ½ jiggers light Jamaica rum
juice of half a ripe lime
1 teaspoon powdered sugar
cracked ice

In a cocktail shaker, blend rum, lime juice and powdered sugar with a good quantity of cracked ice. Shake well and strain into a chilled stemware glass. This drink does not need any garnish.

frozen daiquiri
serves 2 to 3

Frozen Daiquiris can be prepared by adding fresh or frozen fruit or their juices to this basic Frozen Daiquiri recipe. A half of a very ripe banana, for example, or about a third cup mango purée or fully ripe fresh or tinned mangoes, or even some tinned pineapple crush, partially drained, all make superb frozen beverages. Experiment with Frozen Daiquiris by using half light and half dark Jamaica rums and by substituting simple sugar syrup for the powdered sugar listed below.

4 jiggers light Jamaica rum
1 tablespoon fresh lime juice
2 teaspoons powdered sugar
2 cups crushed or shaved ice
maraschino or green cherry (optional)

Place shaved or crushed ice in an electric blender, then add listed ingredients, and blend rather slowly until the mixture is the consistency of snow. Serve at once with a short straw, if desired topped with a maraschino or green cherry. Various fruits can admirably be added to the mixture, as indicated.

el presidente cocktail serves 1

I used to stay at the El Presidente Hotel, in the section of Havana known as Vedado. The following cocktail was said to have been invented there, but I enjoy it here in Jamaica, made with our special local rums, rather than the original Cuban varieties.

1 jigger light Jamaica rum
½ jigger Curaçao
½ jigger dry vermouth
1 dash grenadine syrup
cracked ice

Shake all ingredients together, and strain into a cocktail glass. No garnish is required for this colourful concoction.

davis cocktail serves 1

I really do not know who Davis was, but his or her namesake is a pleasant, highly distinctive cocktail which many people enjoy.

1 jigger dark Jamaica rum
½ jigger dry vermouth
2 dashes raspberry syrup
juice of ½ ripe lime
cracked ice

Shake together all ingredients, and strain into a cocktail glass, to be served without garnish.

aunt mary serves 1

Mr Dermot R. Lunan and his colleagues at the Sheraton—Kingston Hotel have come up with Jamaica's answer to the proverbial Bloody Mary! The drink is increasingly popular as a morning pick-me-up or as a distinctive pleasantry just about any time of the day. Mr Lunan specifies Appleton White Rum for this recipe, and I agree that it is essential for success.

2 ozs Jamaica Appleton White rum
3 ozs tomato juice
Pickapeppa Sauce or Worcestershire Sauce to taste
salt and black pepper to taste
dash or two Tabasco Sauce or hot pepper sauce (optional, but nice)
ice cubes
wedge of fresh, seeded lime

Put ice cubes in a glass, add the Jamaica rum, tomato juice, salt and black pepper, and if desired a dash or two of Tabasco Sauce or hot pepper sauce. Stir gently, and present with a wedge of seeded ripe lime on the rim of the glass.

maude's downfall serves 1

Jamaica's subtly potent White Rum combines artfully with icy-cold tinned grapefruit juice and salt to make this rather new yet increasingly popular weekend beverage. Miss Maude still enjoys it.

2 ozs white Jamaica rum
tinned grapefruit juice, well-chilled
salt to taste
cracked ice

In a tall highball glass, put cracked ice and combine white Jamaica rum and well-chilled canned grapefruit juice. Offer salt shaker, to add to individual taste, plus swizzle stick.

spanish main cocktail
serves 1

My friend and colleague, Mr Jan Blichfeldt, of The Sheraton-Kingston Hotel, has kindly afforded me this recipe for their renowned Spanish Main Cocktail.

2 ozs Appleton Special rum
½ oz dry vermouth
½ oz sweet vermouth
dash of Angostura Bitters
maraschino cherry

Place ice cubes in large old-fashioned glass. Add dash of Bitters, rum, and the two kinds of vermouth. Stir, and garnish with cherry impaled on cocktail stick.

angostura scorpion
serves 1

Scorpions, at least the creepy-crawly variety, are rarely encountered in Jamaica. But their eminently imbibable namesake can be found at many choice bars.

3 tablespoons light Jamaica rum
2 tablespoons simple (sugar) syrup
2 tablespoons strained fresh lime juice
dash of Angostura Bitters
cracked ice

Shake all ingredients together and pour into a chilled cocktail glass. No garnish is necessary.

buccaneer cocktail
serves 1, liberally

The early history of Jamaica found many Buccaneers holding forth both ashore and in the seas around the island. Today these piratical gentlemen are but a memory, and this drink named after them is equally memorable.

1¾ ozs dark Jamaica rum
1¾ ozs light Jamaica rum
1¾ ozs Tia Maria liqueur
6 ozs pineapple juice
crushed ice
2 tablespoons heavy cream
freshly-grated nutmeg

In an electric blender, combine both kinds of rum, the liqueur, and the pineapple juice. Turn mixture into a large goblet or brandy snifter half-filled with crushed ice. Top with heavy cream, sprinkled with nutmeg. Serve with a straw.

jamaica rum fix   serves 1

A fix is not a fizz. It is rather an old-fashioned cocktail, in this instance made with our superlative Jamaica rum—two different varieties, in fact! Very pleasant preprandial sipping, indeed.

1 jigger light Jamaica rum
1 jigger dark Jamaica rum
1 teaspoon granulated sugar
1 teaspoon water
2 teaspoons fresh lime juice
crushed ice
thin slice of ripe lime, or twist of lime peel

In an old-fashioned glass, moisten the sugar with the water. Add the two kinds of Jamaica rum, plus the lime juice, then fill glass with crushed ice and stir gently. Garnish with the thin slice of ripe lime or the twist of lime peel, and serve, with a straw if desired.

goldie's rum fizz   serves 1

Goldie must have been somebody very special, to have such a spectacular fizzy drink named after her! This beverage has considerable local Jamaican reputation as a pick-me-up, but I leave this for you to discover for yourself.

2 jiggers light or white Jamaica rum

1 egg yolk

1 tablespoon powdered sugar

1 jigger or more of fresh lime juice

dash Angostura Bitters

cracked ice

chilled soda water

Thoroughly shake together the Jamaica rum, egg yolk, powdered sugar, lime juice, dash of bitters, and cracked ice. Strain into a tall highball glass, and top with chilled soda water.

pancho's rum fizz   serves 2

Here is a special highly potent rum fizz, named after a fortunate gentleman, Pancho. It is a most refreshing drink and guaranteed to make you feel on top of the world.

1 jigger light Jamaica rum

1 jigger dark Jamaica rum

1 jigger apricot brandy

1 jigger fresh lime juice

1 tablespoon or more granulated sugar

2 tablespoons heavy cream

cracked ice

chilled soda water

Thoroughly shake together the two kinds of rum, apricot brandy, lime juice, sugar, heavy cream and cracked ice, until very well blended and frothy. Strain into 2 chilled highball glasses and top with chilled soda water. No garnish is needed

villa bella fizz   serves 1

Fizzes are fizzy because they are topped with bottled carbonated or soda water. This is a very nice one.

1 oz light Jamaica rum

1 egg white

½ jigger cherry brandy

½ teaspoon granulated sugar

1 tablespoon fresh lime juice

cracked ice

chilled soda water

maraschino cherry

Shake together the rum, egg white, cherry brandy, sugar, lime juice and cracked ice. Strain into a highball glass, top with chilled soda water, and if desired garnish with a red maraschino cherry.

angry bull   serves 1

The Bullshot is a relatively recent arrival on the cocktail scene. Here in Jamaica a variant of it, called the Angry Bull is extremely popular.

1 jigger of light or white Jamaica rum

dash of Pickapeppa or Worcestershire Sauce

dash liquid hot pepper sauce (optional, but customary)

chilled can beef bouillon or consommé

cracked ice

Put rum, Pickapeppa or Worcestershire sauce, liquid hot pepper sauce if desired, in a glass over cracked ice. Fill up the glass with chilled beef consommé or bouillon, stir with a swizzle stick, and serve.

platinum blonde cocktail serves 1

The Platinum Blonde Cocktail is a rather dated one, though still popular with certain ladies who boast of a good collection of wigs or wiglets.

1 jigger light Jamaica rum
1 jigger Cointreau
½ jigger cream
cracked ice
green maraschino cherry (optional)

Combine rum, Cointreau, and cream with cracked ice, and shake well. Strain into cocktail glass, and if desired garnish with green maraschino cherry on a cocktail stick.

naked lady cocktail serves 3 naked or plain ladies, or gentlemen

Now my idea of a memorable sight would be to encounter a naked lady, standing in the full glow of incredible Jamaican moonlight on one of our sugar-white beaches, daintily sipping a Naked Lady Cocktail. Such somewhat dubious delights are not, unfortunately, guaranteed to visitors by the Jamaica Tourist Board, though I understand they are reviewing the situation.

3 jiggers light or white Jamaica rum
2 jiggers sweet vermouth
4 dashes apricot brandy
2 dashes grenadine syrup
4 dashes fresh lime or lemon juice
cracked ice

Combine all ingredients, and shake well, to strain into chilled cocktail glasses. Serve, if possible, on a Jamaican beach on a full moonlight night.

portland cocktail serves 1

This delectable cocktail is the invention of a crony of mine in the glorious Jamaican Parish of Portland. He, like me, enjoys his Jamaica rum in just about any form, but especially this way.

1 jigger light Jamaica rum
1 jigger Dubonnet
4 dashes orange bitters
cracked ice
twist of ripe lime peel

Stir rum, Dubonnet, and bitters until well chilled with ice, and serve strained in chilled cocktail glass with twist of ripe lime peel.

harbour street cocktail serves 1

Rose's Lime Juice is a special Caribbean delight and combines pleasantly with prime light Jamaica rums of several varieties to create this drink which is designed for leisurely sipping.

1 ½ to 2 ozs light Jamaica rum
¾ oz Rose's Lime Juice
ice cubes
twist of lime peel

Mix light Jamaica rum with Rose's Lime Juice gently and serve over ice cubes in an old-fashioned glass garnished with a twist of lime peel.

jamaican martini　serves 1

In Kingston and Montego Bay and Port Antonio and Ocho Rios, this delightful Jamaican rum cocktail is an increasingly popular luncheon drink. Serve it icy cold.

2 ozs light Jamaica rum
¼ to ½ oz dry sherry
cracked ice
twist of lime peel, or stuffed green olive

Stir Jamaica rum with sherry and cracked ice until very cold, but do not allow the mixture to be diluted. Strain into a pre-chilled martini glass and serve with a twist of lime peel or stuffed green olive.

egg nog　serves 24

Egg Nog is a traditional beverage, most often served around the Christmas and New Year holiday seasons. It is not, though, necessary nor obligatory to restrict the offering of this drink to this time of the year. By using the following easy recipe, Egg Nog can be presented with pride all the year round. Try it soon, for your next festive home get-together.

1 bottle (fifth) light Jamaica rum
12 egg yolks
½ lb granulated sugar
1 quart whole milk
1 quart heavy cream whipped until stiff but not dry
freshly grated Jamaica nutmeg

Put the egg yolks in a large bowl and beat until they are light in colour. Then gradually add the sugar, and beat until mixture thickens. Stir in the milk and the Jamaica rum. Chill, covered, for 3 to 4 hours. Pour into a pre-chilled punch-bowl, and fold in the whipped cream. Dust with freshly grated nutmeg.

rum collins　serves 1

We enjoy many different kinds of Rum Collins. Here is a basic recipe for this popular, cooling, tall drink, and following, some suggested additions.

1½ ozs Jamaica rum of your choice, usually light
1 oz fresh lime juice
1 oz simple syrup
cracked ice
carbonated soda water
slice of unpeeled seeded orange impaled with maraschino cherry

In a cocktail shaker, combine rum, lime juice, simple syrup, and cracked ice, and shake very thoroughly. Strain into tall collins glass, add some of the ice if desired, and top off with carbonated soda water. Garnish with slice of unpeeled seeded orange impaled with maraschino cherry.

variations and additions : for each drink, during mixing, add, to taste, fresh orange juice, tinned grapefruit juice, tamarind nectar, guava nectar, apple cider or mango nectar.

rum with tonic　serves 1

Light Jamaica rums with quinine water or tonic, adorned with a wedge of seeded ripe lime, are justifiably popular drinks throughout Jamaica.

1½ ozs light Jamaica rum
quinine water or tonic water
cracked ice
wedge of seeded ripe lime

In a tall highball glass, combine light Jamaica rum with quinine water or tonic, over cracked ice to taste. Serve with seeded lime wedge on rim of glass.

rum swizzle   serves 1

One of Jamaica's most popular indigenous rum drinks is the Rum Swizzle. Here is my favourite version, which can of course be adapted to individual taste, without difficulty.

1 oz light Jamaica rum
½ oz fresh lime juice
¼ oz simple syrup
1 dash Angostura Bitters
cracked ice
carbonated soda water

In a cocktail shaker, combine lime juice, simple syrup, bitters, and the Jamaica rum, with cracked ice to taste. Shake very thoroughly, until frothy, and without delay turn into a high-ball glass. Fill up glass with chilled soda water, and if desired garnish with a maraschino cherry.

salome cocktail   serves 2

Somebody with a good Jamaican sense of humour invented this Salome Cocktail. Try it and see its effect!

2 jiggers dark Jamaica rum
1 jigger crême de banane
¼ jigger fresh lime juice
¼ jigger simple syrup
cracked ice
thick slice ripe banana stuck with maraschino cherry

Shake together the rum, banana liqueur, lime juice, simple syrup and cracked ice. Strain into chilled champagne glass or other stemware, and serve garnished with banana slice stuck with red cherry.

stony hill special   serves 1

Mexico may have invented the magnificent tequila Margarita, but here in Jamaica we have evolved our own special version, a tasteful one featuring our unique White Rum. Be sure that your cocktail glasses are thoroughly chilled prior to serving.

1½ ozs white Jamaica rum
¼ oz Triple Sec
1 oz fresh lime juice
additional lime juice
salt
crushed ice

Rub well-chilled cocktail glass with fresh lime juice, then dredge in salt, by turning upside down on a paper napkin sprinkled with salt. Combine white Jamaica rum, Triple Sec, and 1 oz fresh lime juice in a cocktail shaker with crushed ice, and shake thoroughly until almost frothy. Strain carefully into prepared glass and serve at once.

jamaica screwdriver serves 1

In Jamaica, we have a term called 'screwdriver industry,' which rather irreverently designates a local company which might produce the metal part of the screwdriver, but neglects to furnish the customers with any sort of handle for its use. More felicitously, we also have a Jamaica Screwdriver, which is a tall and cooling beverage featuring, as one might expect, one of our Jamaica rums.

1 to 2 ozs white Jamaica rum
fresh orange juice
cracked ice
wedge of ripe seeded lime

In tall highball glass, over cracked ice, stir white Jamaica rum and fresh orange juice. Place seeded lime wedge on rim of glass and serve at once.

jamaica rum sour serves 1

A good tart Rum Sour is a pleasure on a warm Jamaican afternoon. And it is too good to be ignored at other times, on cooler days!

1½ ozs light Jamaica rum
1 oz fresh lime juice
¾ oz simple syrup
cracked ice
thin slice seeded ripe lime
maraschino cherry

In a cocktail shaker, combine rum, lime juice, and simple syrup with cracked ice. Shake thoroughly until almost frothy, and strain into chilled sour glass. Garnish glass rim with thin slice of lime, and drop a maraschino cherry into the drink.

hot rum toddy serves 1

I really do not know why Hot Rum Toddy is a drink destined, according to Caribbean and other tradition, to be served only on chilly holidays, particularly around the Christmas and New Year season. But this hearty brew is refreshing even on warm evenings, and is marvellous for warding off an incipient attack of the ague.

1 to 2 jiggers white or light Jamaica rum
1 teaspoon honey (preferably Jamaica logwood)
1 lemon or lime slice, impaled with 4 whole cloves
boiling water
stick cinnamon bark

In a heavy mug or cup, dissolve the honey in a little hot water, stirring constantly. Blend in the Jamaica rum of your choice, then add the lemon or lime slice stuck with the whole cloves. Fill up mug or cup with boiling water, and add the stick of cinnamon bark.

myers original jamaica egg nog serves 20

Everyone, particularly at the festive Holiday Season, enjoys a good hearty Rum Egg Nog. Here is an exceptional one, from the makers of Myers Rum.

1 bottle (fifth) Myers rum
12 egg yolks
½ lb granulated sugar
1 quart whole milk
1 quart heavy cream
freshly-grated nutmeg

Beat egg yolks with rotary beater until light. Add the sugar, and continue to beat until mixture is thick and pale in colour. Gradually stir in the milk and the dark rum, and chill in refrigerator for 3 hours, stirring often. Turn mixture into a punch bowl, fold in the heavy cream which has been whipped until stiff, and place in refrigerator for an additional one hour. Serve sprinkled with freshly grated Jamaica nutmeg.

hot rum and cider serves 1

Have you ever enjoyed the delights of Hot Rum and Cider? If not, then you are missing a refreshing and interesting beverage, guaranteed to prove a hit at your next party on a cool evening.

1½ jiggers white or light Jamaica rum
1 teaspoon cane or maple syrup
1 teaspoon granulated sugar
1 tablespoon fresh lime or lemon juice
1 lime or lemon slice, impaled with 2 whole cloves
hot apple cider

In a heavy mug or large cup, mix the Jamaica rum, syrup, granulated sugar and lime or lemon juice. Add lime or lemon slice, stuck with whole cloves, and fill mug or cup with hot apple cider, to serve.

tom-and-jerry   serves 1

Have you ever considered who such people as Tom and Jerry might have been? In recent years they are best known as a hilarious cat and mouse animated cartoon, but for Jamaica rum connoisseurs, they combine their names and their reputation to give us a luscious, bracing drink!

| 1 jigger light or white Jamaica rum |
| 1 egg yolk |
| 1 teaspoon powdered sugar |
| ¼ teaspoon ground Jamaica allspice (pimento) |
| 1 egg white |
| hot milk |
| freshly-grated nutmeg |

In a small bowl, beat the egg yolk then beat in the sugar, allspice (called pimento in Jamaica), and the Jamaica rum of your choice. Continue to beat until smooth and thickened. In another bowl, beat the egg white for a few seconds, then blend into the rum mixture. Turn into pre-heated mug or large cup, fill with hot milk, mix thoroughly, dust with nutmeg and serve at once.

rum bullock   serves 2

A Rum Bullock sounds like rather a forceful drink and indeed this is the case! This requires the use of true coconut milk, for which a recipe is appended.

| 2 jiggers light, white, or dark Jamaica rum |
| 2 cups coconut milk (see recipe) |
| 2 drops vanilla extract |
| 1 pinch ground Jamaica allspice (pimento) |
| dash Angostura bitters |
| cracked ice |

Shake together all the ingredients until thoroughly blended and frothy. Strain into a chilled glass, and serve particularly as an early morning pick-you-up.

coconut milk

Here is the recipe for true Coconut Milk. Ideally a fresh, dry coconut should be used.

| 2 cups freshly-grated or moist packaged coconut flesh |
| 3 cups water |

If using a fresh dry coconut, break shell, peel off the dark outer skin and grate the flesh from the outside in. This gives more body to the coconut. Put the grated coconut and the water in a saucepan and bring to a quick boil. Stir often, then remove from heat and allow to stand for 30 minutes. Using your hands, squeeze out the liquid, straining it if desired, to remove all tiny bits of coconut flesh. This heavy liquid is true coconut milk, the watery fluid found inside the coconut being correctly known as coconut water.

hot buttered rum   serves 1

One of the most pleasurable evenings I have spent in Jamaica was high on a promontory near Newcastle, where my host served us a special array of indigenous appetisers such as codfish stamp-and-go, and a bountiful supply of Hot Buttered Rum, served in heirloom pewter mugs. We watched the incredible sparkling lights of Kingston far below, and felt at ease with our special Jamaican world.

| 1 jigger white, light, or dark Jamaica rum |
| 1 teaspoon brown or white sugar |
| small piece cinnamon stick |
| pinch ground allspice or nutmeg |
| boiling water |
| butter |

In pre-heated mug or large heavy cup, dissolve brown or white sugar in a little water. Stir in the Jamaica rum of your choice. Add the piece of cinnamon stick, plus either ground allspice (Jamaica pimento) or nutmeg, and fill up with boiling water. Top with a goodly pat of butter and serve at once.

jamaican gold doubloons serves 6

Today, during the explorations at Port Royal, gold doubloons are periodically uncovered by the underwater divers who probe the ruins brought about by seventeenth-century earthquakes. Here is a special frozen drink which Henry Morgan and all his cronies would have enjoyed back in Old Port Royal.

½ cup light Jamaica rum
¾ cup fresh orange juice
juice of 1 ripe lime
1 teaspoon sugar
¼ cup orange liqueur
4 cups finely-crushed ice
sprig of fresh mint (optional)

Whirl all ingredients, except mint sprigs in an electric blender, and serve either in an old-fashioned or stemware glass. Garnish with mint, if desired.

blue mountain punch makes about 12 glasses

Mary Slater's attractive book, *Caribbean Cooking for Pleasure* (Hamlyn, London, 1970), contains some interesting rum recipes, including this one, which she says 'is the punch to drink on the high peaks in the cool early morning.'

½ cup light or dark Jamaica rum
1 tablespoon powdered ginger
1 teaspoon grated nutmeg
7½ cups warmed beer
3 eggs
2 tablespoons molasses

Blend the ginger and nutmeg with 6¾ cups of the beer and heat. Beat the eggs with the remaining beer and molasses. Add the warm beer to the egg mixture a little at a time, beating all the time. Add the rum and serve at once.

planter's punch serves 1

A Planter's Punch seems, for many visitors to our luxuriant island, to be the very epitome of tropical leisure. Every good bartender has his own personal, subtle variations, as do private individuals in their own homes. Here is a recipe which I personally enjoy very much and the reader can take off from here, adding or subtracting to individual taste. Jamaica rum and fresh fruit juices are of course absolutely obligatory.

1 jigger light Jamaica rum
1 jigger dark Jamaica rum
2 jiggers fresh orange juice
½ jigger fresh lime juice
simple syrup to taste
cracked ice
garnish of unpeeled orange slice, impaled with peeled finger of ripe pineapple and maraschino cherry for a topping.

Shake both kinds of Jamaica rum with fruit juices, simple sugar syrup to taste, and cracked ice, and pour into a tall, pre-chilled collins glass. Garnish as indicated and serve with straws.

philadelphia fish house punch
makes about 50 servings

One of the most impressive of rum punches which I enjoy has long been a speciality in Philadelphia, U.S.A. and named after the well-known Fish House there. Dark Jamaica rum is generally called for in this traditional recipe, but you may like to use half and half dark and light, as I prefer for home use.

½ bottle (fifth) dark Jamaica rum, or ¼ bottle (fifth) dark and ¼ bottle (fifth) light Jamaica rum, combined
1 bottle (fifth) brandy
1 jigger peach brandy
2 cups brown sugar
2 quarts water
peel and juice of 6 ripe lemons

In a large heavy pot, heat sugar and water together until sugar has completely dissolved, stirring often with a wooden spoon. Add lemon peel and juice, plus Jamaica rum, brandy and peach brandy. Mix well, remove from heat and allow to stand for several hours to mellow. Strain over a large block of ice, about an hour prior to serving to chill well, and dilute slightly. Serve in chilled punch cups.

jamaica grand punch
serves about 30 persons

Grand bowls of punch frequently appear at festive Jamaican gatherings. Many of these crystal-cut glass sets are heirlooms of great antiquity! On occasion, these are proudly filled with the following punch.

1½ quarts dark Jamaica rum
1½ quarts unsweetened pineapple juice
3 large tins mango nectar
1 cup lime juice
block of ice
soda water to taste
garnish with slim fingers of fresh peeled pineapple

In your prettiest big punch bowl, combine the dark Jamaican rum, pineapple juice, mango nectar, and lime juice, pouring it over a block of ice. Add the soda water to taste, garnish with pineapple fingers, and serve.

hot spiced cider   serves 4

Apple cider is very popular in Jamaica, being imported for the most part from England, because our mountain apples are not very successful or common. Here is an interesting way with cider, to be served hot when enjoying the cool evenings in our glorious Blue Mountains.

¾ cup light Jamaica rum
1 quart apple cider
¼ cup granulated sugar
⅛ teaspoon salt
1 cinnamon stick, broken up
12 whole cloves
8 whole allspice (pimento berries)

Combine all the ingredients except Jamaica rum in a large saucepan, and bring to the boil. Cool and let stand for at least 4 hours, stirring occasionally. Strain and reheat to serve, stirring in the Jamaica rum at last moment. Serve in large mugs, if possible.

jamaica rummy ginger beer
serves 1

Home-made ginger beer is a particular delight in many parts of Jamaica and is often fiery to the taste. For the non-initiate, I recommend this somewhat subdued version of a very refreshing drink!

1 jigger white or light Jamaica rum
1 can well-chilled ginger beer
cracked ice
candied (preserved) ginger (optional)

Put the rum and chilled ginger beer in a tall glass over the cracked ice, stirring gently with a swizzle stick. If desired, impale a piece of candied (preserved) ginger on a long cocktail stick and place across the top of the glass.

piña colada   serves 6

Piña Colada, pronounced *peen*-ya koe-*lah*-da, has long been a great favourite in many parts of the American tropics, from South Florida and Cuba southwards. Yet, it has never been common here in Jamaica, where our lovely rums make it exceptional!

⅔ cup light or dark Jamaica rum
½ cup coconut milk (see page 21)
1 cup Jamaica tinned pineapple juice, chilled
2 cups crushed ice
fingers of ripe Jamaica pineapple, speared with maraschino cherry

Thoroughly chill 6 cocktail glasses. In an electric blender, combine Jamaica rum, coconut milk, pineapple juice, and ice. Blend at high speed for 30 seconds. Pour into chilled glasses, and add garnish of pineapple fingers with impaled maraschino cherry.

john's mango masterpiece
makes about 10 cocktails

To prepare mango purée, essential for John's Mango Masterpiece, whirl either fresh peeled fibreless ripe fruit or drained tinned ones, in your electric blender until smooth. Then proceed. And serve with some caution, since as John discovered, this is a notably powerful and delectable beverage!

1 cup light Jamaica rum, chilled
1 cup mango purée, chilled
¼ cup or more fresh strained lime juice, chilled
¼ cup or more water, chilled
sugar or simple syrup to taste
crushed ice

Have all the ingredients, including mango purée (see introductory paragraph) very well chilled prior to assembling this recipe. Blend all ingredients in an electric blender with crushed ice until smooth and very cold. Serve in small amounts in chilled stemware cocktail glasses, without garnish.

hot rum mocha   serves 6

I first enjoyed this superlative Hot Rum Mocha beverage several years ago in a handsome old home, overlooking the sprawling, glittering lights of Kingston. It was a cool evening, and sips of the rich drink from the heavy pewter mugs were much appreciated as we watched the magnificent views.

3 jiggers light or dark Jamaica rum
1 package semi-sweet chocolate bits
6 cups whole milk
3 tablespoons very strong cold coffee
1 cup heavy whipping cream
2 teaspoons powdered sugar
6 tablespoons thick cream

In a heavy and preferably non-sticking saucepan, melt the chocolate bits and the 6 cups milk and strong cold coffee over a medium heat, stirring constantly. Whip the heavy cream, blending in the Jamaica rum and powdered sugar, and keep this chilled until serving time. To serve, place 1 tablespoon thick cream in bottom of each cup or mug, fill with mocha mixture, and top with rum-flavoured whipped cream.

strawberry-rum tipsop serves 1

Many Jamaicans are very fond of colourful, sweet fruit bottled syrups, which are sold in every shop throughout the island. Here is a pleasant, not quite so sweet way to use commercial strawberry syrup.

1 jigger light or white Jamaica rum
½ jigger bottled strawberry syrup
½ jigger or more fresh lime juice
crushed ice
chilled ginger ale

In a tall highball glass, mix together the Jamaica rum, strawberry syrup, and lime juice. Add crushed ice, and fill up glass with chilled ginger ale, preferably the spicy Jamaican variety!

jamaica banana slush serves 2

Here is a refreshing and elegant Jamaica rum drink, which ideally should be consumed and enjoyed while seated under a full Caribbean moon, with an extra-special friend.

3 ozs Appleton Punch rum
2 tablespoons fresh lime juice
2 tablespoons unsweetened pineapple juice
1 ripe Jamaica banana, thinly sliced
simple syrup or granulated sugar to taste
crushed ice
pieces of fresh or tinned pineapple
red or green maraschino cherries

Using your electric blender, add the Jamaica Punch rum, lime and pineapple juices, the banana, simple syrup or sugar, and enough crushed ice to fill container about one-half full. Blend until just slushy. Pour at once into two well-chilled stem glasses of your choice, and garnish with skewers made by impaling first one piece of pineapple, then a maraschino cherry, then another piece of pineapple turned in the opposite direction to bottom one.

iced tea montego bay

Everybody enjoys a tall frosty glass of iced tea during the warm weather especially here in Jamaica. It is very enjoyable if prepared in the following special fashion.

1 or 1 ½ jiggers of light, or white or dark Jamaica rum
iced tea
ice cubes
sugar
fresh lime or lemon wedges

Put ice cubes and rum into a pre-chilled glass. Then pour in your favourite version iced tea, mix, stir and serve with pride! Sugar and fresh lime or lemon wedges can be offered as accompaniments. A hint: Do not chill your prepared tea because it may become cloudy. Prepare it according to your favourite recipe, keep covered in a cool but not chilly place and pour over ice cubes when ready to serve.

mocha-rum delight makes about 8 cups

When holidaying in Jamaica's glorious mountains, a warming drink is often most welcome especially at night when the temperature can dip down rather low! Here is a favourite hearty beverage with many of us, which is as well appropriate at sea-level.

1 cup light Jamaica rum, warmed
4 cups extra-strong hot cocoa, made with milk
1 ½ cups strong hot Blue Mountain coffee
1 cup heavy cream, whipped, with
1 tablespoon granulated sugar

Beat together the rum, cocoa, and coffee. Fold in the sweetened whipped cream, and serve without a moment's delay in heated mugs.

tamarind lindo   serves 4

The Tamarind is one of our more unusual Jamaican fruits, being utilised as a special tart seasoning in chutneys, in certain special main dishes and especially in drinks. Tinned Tamarind nectar is very refreshing, especially when combined with Jamaica rum and a ripe banana as in the following recipe by my horticulture and culinary colleague, Mr Edward A. Flickinger.

4 ozs light Jamaica rum
1 cup tinned tamarind nectar
1 ripe banana
1 ½ tablespoons granulated sugar
⅛ teaspoon ground allspice (Jamaican pimento)
crushed ice
fresh rinsed flowers for garnish (optional)

Using an electric blender whirl at low speed the rum, nectar, banana, sugar and allspice. Then add enough crushed ice to chill but not dilute the mixture. Blend again and serve in a pre-chilled sour or other stemglass. If desired, garnish each serving with a rinsed tropical flower, such as a frangipani, or small hibiscus, or bougainvillea (no oleanders, as these are poisonous!).

**inventive cookery with
jamaica rum**

iced rum soup   serves 4 to 6

Utilising our luscious Jamaica rum, we have a rather remarkable preliminary course for the gourmet menu, a cold soup. If possible, the chilled bowls should be presented at table on a bed of crushed ice.

2 or more tablespoons dark Jamaica rum
2 10-oz cans beef consommé
2 teaspoons finely-chopped green scallion tops
wafer-thin slices fresh lime

Combine the rum with the tinned beef consommé (choose the gelatin added variety), and place in refrigerator overnight. Stir occasionally, until it jells thoroughly. Serve each portion in a chilled small soup bowl or cup, sprinkled with scallion tops, and topped by a twisted thin slice of fresh lime.

rumona appetizer dip

Using Jamaica's unique and delectable Rumona Liqueur, we have a very distinctive appetiser dip, to be served at cocktail time with an assortment of crisp crackers and slim sticks of fresh ripe pineapple.

2 to 3 tablespoons Rumona Liqueur
2 large (8-oz) packages cream cheese, softened
¼ to ½ cup coarsely-shredded sharp Cheddar cheese
heavy cream as necessary
assorted crisp crackers
chilled slender fingers of fresh ripe pineapple

Cream the softened cream cheese and Cheddar cheese together, and add Rumona to taste, plus enough heavy cream to make a spreadable dip. The mixture must not be soupy in texture! Turn into an attractive serving bowl, chill well, and serve with assorted crisp crackers and chilled pineapple sticks.

sausage-pineapple kebabs serves 12 or more as appetizers

These little hot kebabs or kabobs are exceptionally popular in Jamaica at cocktail time. Just about any sort of spicy sausages can be utilised, but I prefer the sweet Italian ones whenever I can find them. Spanish or Mexican chorizos are lovely, too.

2 tablespoons dark or light Jamaica rum
1 lb sweet Italian sausage, or chorizos, or other firm spicy sausage
3 to 4 tablespoons butter
1 large tin (about 16 oz) pineapple chunks, drained
Toothpicks or small cocktail bamboo skewers

Cut sausages of your choice into 1-inch pieces, and in a heavy skillet sauté them in the butter until nicely browned on all sides, turning as needed with slotted spoon. When all sausage pieces are cooked, add Jamaica rum to skillet, cover, and simmer for just a few minutes over very low heat. Add drained pineapple chunks, mix in, re-cover the skillet, and allow to heat through. Impale a piece of sausage and a piece of pineapple on each toothpick or preferably small cocktail bamboo skewers, and serve while hot.

rummy appetizer sausages

Sausages and Jamaica rum go very well together! This may seem like an unusual combination of flavours, but once you have tried the following delicacy, which originated in Portugal but which has in recent years found considerable popularity with many of us here in the Caribbean, I feel certain that you will agree. Lovely for cocktail time, with your favourite Jamaica rum drink as an accompaniment for leisurely conversational entertaining.

5 to 6 ozs white or light Jamaica rum
1 pound spicy sausage, such as Polish, Portuguese, Italian, or Spanish chorizo
French, Italian, or Cuban bread, sliced very thinly
red radishes, sliced thickly, chilled

Place sausages of your choice in a large saucepan, add enough hot water just to cover, and simmer for about 15 minutes. Drain, remove skins from sausages, and cut into one-inch pieces. Place these pieces in a skillet, warm through, then add the warmed rum, and ignite with a match. When flames die down, transfer rum-flavoured sausage pieces to a heated serving dish, with cocktail sticks, thin slices of crusty bread, and chilled thick radish slices in side dishes. Impale a piece of hot sausage, wrap it in a slice of bread with one of radish, and they are ready to serve.

jamaica honey-rum shrimp
serves 4 to 6

Some years ago, I published a Shrimp Cookbook, containing some 140 different ways to prepare this lovely crustacean. This may seem like a rather large number of methods of serving shrimps, yet scarcely a week passes that I do not come upon a new way to cook them! Here, for example, is a recently discovered delight, combining shrimp with our glorious Jamaica rum, and our island's special logwood honey, too. (Other sorts of honey can, of course, be substituted, if the superb logwood variety is unavailable.)

This culinary epic should be served with hot fluffy rice, a salad of thinly-sliced ripe tomatoes and cucumber which have been marinated in olive oil and fresh lime juice with a touch of salt and black pepper, and if the event is as festive as the recipe warrants, a bottle of chilled white or rosé wine.

Ideally, the shrimps should be broiled over charcoal, for added flavour, but they can of course be done under pre-heated broiler or on the kitchen stove.

¼ cup dark or light Jamaica rum
1 lb medium, raw shrimp, shelled
¼ cup Jamaica logwood honey
½ teaspoon minced fresh ginger root
bamboo or metal skewers, 9 inches long

In a heavy saucepan, combine the rum, honey and fresh ginger root and heat through, stirring constantly. Pour this mixture over the shelled shrimp in a large shallow bowl, and marinate them. Allow shrimp to cool for about 2 hours in a refrigerator and turn shrimp in marinade frequently. Skewer shrimp, sideways with the heads doubled up against the tails and put about 4 shrimps on each skewer. Broil over a good hot bed of charcoal. Brush on the marinade during broiling, until the shrimp are well glazed and cooked. This usually takes about 10 minutes. Serve promptly, on the skewers.

rum french toast   serves 4

A tasty and easy breakfast or brunch dish, which is all too seldom encountered in Jamaica, is French Toast. I make mine a special way by adding a dollop of Jamaica rum at the last moment and serving the pieces of crusty bread piping hot with scrambled eggs, broiled back bacon, logwood honey and accompanied by Blue Mountain coffee. See what you think!

1 tablespoon dark Jamaica rum
2 large eggs, lightly beaten
⅔ cup of milk
¼ teaspoon salt
⅛ teaspoon ground allspice
8 slices firm white bread, trimmed of crusts, cut into halves
2 to 4 tablespoons butter

Prepare the bread, trimming away all the crust and cut into neat halves lengthwise. In a large bowl, blend together the eggs, milk, salt and allspice but do not beat. Fold in the Jamaica rum at the last moment, then dip the bread halves into this mixture, drain briefly and place in a sizeable skillet in which the butter has been melted over a medium flame. Brown one side of the bread slice, then carefully turn with a spatula and brown on the other side. Repeat until all the bread pieces are done, removing the pieces as they are cooked and keeping hot.

sweet scrambled rice serves 4 to 6

For the next elegant brunch at your home, consider serving your family and guests the following rice dish, flavoured with Jamaica rum and other tasty ingredients. I like this distinctive recipe with baked eggs and frizzled ham slices, and of course lots of hot coffee. Very tropical, and very nice!

¼ cup light or white Jamaica rum
¼ cup seedless raisins
1 cup raw long grain rice
¼ teaspoon salt
1 cup granulated sugar
3 cups milk
2 tablespoons coarsely-chopped cashews or peanuts
grated rind (zest) of a ripe lemon
1 egg, beaten
¼ cup butter
¼ cup granulated sugar
¼ teaspoon or more ground allspice (Jamaican pimento)

Soak raisins in Jamaica rum for several hours. In top of double boiler over boiling water, cook the rice with the salt and 1 cup sugar and the milk, for 30 minutes or until rice is tender and milk absorbed. Stir occasionally with a wooden spoon. Add drained raisins, nuts, lemon zest, and the beaten egg, mixing gently but thoroughly. In sizeable skillet, melt butter and add rice mixture, to sauté until brown crust forms on bottom. Carefully turn and brown upper side. Serve while hot, sprinkled with a combination of sugar and ground allspice.

carib cocktail balls

Here is a nice easy and attractive sweet appetiser and one which is rather different. You may wish to serve these cocktail balls impaled on a plain or coloured cocktail stick stuck into a whole grapefruit and set on a pretty special platter.

1 teaspoon dark Jamaica rum
⅓ cup tinned crushed pineapple, well drained
1 large 8-oz package creamed cheese, softened
2 tablespoons mayonnaise
⅓ cup finely chopped cashews, pecans or other nuts

In a bowl, mix the Jamaica rum with the pineapple, softened creamed cheese and mayonnaise until very thoroughly blended. There should be enough residual juice from the pineapple to do this. Form into balls one inch in diameter and roll in chopped nuts to coat evenly on all sides. Place in freezing compartment of your refrigerator until very firm and cold, but not frozen. This usually takes about 15 or 20 minutes. Serve on cocktail sticks which can, if desired, be impaled on a whole grapefruit for attractive presentation.

lobster rio nuevo   serves 4

Superb Caribbean spiny lobster is frequently available in Jamaica, and it should be presented at table as quickly as possible, since this unique thorny crustacean quickly loses all of its gastronomic charm. An exceptional way to treat flapping-fresh lobsters from our island's seas is in the following fashion. Offer this gourmet dish either alongside or over hot fluffy rice or on crisp freshly-made toast points, with a light salad of lettuce, tomato wedges, and cucumber fingers in an oil-and-vinegar dressing. I like to serve a rosé or dry white wine, well-chilled, with such a glorious repast.

3 tablespoons light Jamaica rum
4 cups 1-inch cubes freshly-cooked lobster
½ cup ground lean pork
4 tablespoons butter
3 tablespoons minced green scallion tops
2 tablespoons flour
½ teaspoon salt
¼ teaspoon freshly-ground black pepper
¼ teaspoon paprika
2 or more drops hot pepper sauce
1½ cups whole milk

In a large heavy saucepan, over medium heat, sauté the ground lean pork (the meat from a couple of good pork chops will usually suffice) in 2 of the tablespoons of butter, stirring often, until almost brown. Add the green scallion tops and continue to stir. Cook until the pork is brown and crumbly. Remove the saucepan from the heat. In another smaller saucepan, melt the other 2 tablespoons of butter, stir in the flour, salt, black pepper and paprika. Cook, still stirring, for 3 or 4 minutes over a very low heat. Add the hot pepper sauce. Do not add too much! Gradually stir in the milk, cooking and stirring after each addition until a good smooth sauce is obtained. Stir in the rum and mix through. Turn the contents of this saucepan into the saucepan containing the browned pork, return to the heat and bring almost to the boil. Do not let it boil completely or else the flavour will be ruined. Add the cooked lobster cubes to this special sauce and just heat through. Serve without delay with rice or toast.

rum chicken bites
serves 6 to 8 as an appetizer

Here is a succulent way with boned, bite-size pieces of chicken, batter-fried and served either as an hors d'œuvre or main entrée for a light supper, with hot rice and perhaps an avocado salad. It combines the concepts of both Oriental and Jamaican cookery and is delightful!

2 tablespoons dark or 3 tablespoons light Jamaica rum
1 large or 2 small frying chickens
2 tablespoons soy sauce
½ teaspoon granulated sugar
½ teaspoon freshly-grated ginger root
1 cup all-purpose flour
2 tablespoons cornstarch (cornflour)
1 large fresh egg
about ¾ cup of water
deep hot fat or oil for frying

Using a sharp knife, carefully cut the chicken, (including some of the skin, if desired, as this is very tasty), off the bones, reserving the excess skin and remnants for later use in a soup. Cut chicken pieces into bite-size chunks, about an inch or more in all directions. In a large bowl combine the Jamaica rum, soy sauce and grated ginger root. Add the chicken pieces and mix well and allow to marinate for one hour. In another bowl, mix the flour, cornstarch, egg and enough water to make a thin batter. Mix thoroughly and allow to stand for 10 minutes or so in the refrigerator. Drain the pieces of chicken from the marinade, dip them into the batter and fry them, a few at a time in deep hot fat or oil that has been heated to about 375°F. Fry until they are nicely browned, remove with a slotted spoon and drain well on absorbent paper towels. Serve without delay while very hot!

cockpit country chicken
serves 4 liberally

There are so many ingenious and delicious methods of preparing chicken that it would seem, at first glance, that all of the recipes had long since been utilised! But here is one which I have never encountered outside my own kitchen and I believe it is unique, as is the extraordinary part of Jamaica after which it is named.

I offer my Cockpit Country Chicken with either baked yams or mashed Irish potatoes and chochoes cooked in a little salted water, then cubed and liberally dressed with butter and freshly-ground black pepper. I also serve a salad of thinly-sliced ripe tomatoes liberally sprinkled with olive oil, fresh lime juice, oregano, salt and black pepper and marinated in the refrigerator for an hour or so.

3 tablespoons light Jamaica rum
1 large frying chicken, cut into quarters
2 tablespoons olive oil
2 tablespoons butter
½ cup thinly-sliced onion
1 small clove garlic, peeled, minced
¼ cup slivered sweet green pepper
¼ cup diced, peeled green tomato
1 teaspoon salt
½ teaspoon freshly-ground black pepper
pinch ground allspice (pimento)
2 cups cooked, drained, minced callaloo (or spinach)
2 large hard boiled eggs

Using a large heavy skillet with cover, or Dutch oven, fry the chicken quarters in a mixture of the oil and butter. Cook two pieces of chicken at a time and turn as needed with tongs, until well browned on all sides. Remove the pieces as they are cooked and keep them warm. When the chicken is cooked put the onion, garlic, and green pepper in the skillet and cook, stirring often, over a medium heat until soft but not browned. Add the green tomato, salt, black pepper, and allspice and continue to cook, stirring occasionally with a wooden spoon until all vegetables are just soft. Return the chicken pieces to the mixture, stir in the callaloo or spinach, mix well, cover skillet and simmer over lowest heat turning chicken occasionally until this is tender. Blend in the Jamaica rum and cook uncovered for a few minutes. Meanwhile, mash the yolks and the whites of hard boiled eggs separately. Serve each portion of the hot chicken with a good amount of the green gravy, which will be very tasty. Top with a separated sprinkling of both egg yolks and whites.

beef balls in rum-coffee-pawpaw sauce
serves 4 liberally

The following Beef Balls in Rum-Coffee-Pawpaw Sauce are indeed exciting, and can be served either as distinctive hot appetisers, or as the entrée for a special tropical menu. For the latter, I would suggest accompanying the meat balls with hot fluffy buttered rice, a nice crisp tossed green salad with your favourite dressing, heated thick slices of crusty bread, and a light dessert, perhaps a piece of fine cheese and crisp water biscuits. Served as hors d'œuvre, offer your guests small fresh toast rounds or crisp crackers, cocktail sticks, and plenty of napkins!

2 tablespoons dark, or 3 tablespoons light Jamaica rum
1½ lbs coarsely-ground lean beef
2 tablespoons finely-chopped onion
1 tablespoon finely-chopped green scallion tops
1 tablespoon finely-chopped sweet green pepper
½ cup coarse fresh bread crumbs
1 large fresh egg
3 tablespoons butter
2 tablespoons cooking oil
1 tablespoon granulated sugar
2 cups strong hot Jamaica coffee
¼ cup cream
1 cup diced peeled ripe pawpaw (papaya)
salt to taste
additional slices of peeled ripe pawpaw for garnish, uncooked

In a large bowl, gently but thoroughly combine the beef, onion, scallion tops, green pepper, breadcrumbs and egg. Do not overmix! Form gently into neat balls about one inch in diameter, and if possible refrigerate, covered with waxed paper or foil, for about 30 minutes. In large heavy skillet with cover, heat the butter and oil together, and over medium heat thoroughly brown the meat balls on all sides, a few at a time, to avoid overcrowding. Remove balls carefully when cooked with a slotted spoon, and keep them warm. Drain off fat from skillet, and reduce heat to simmer. Dissolve the sugar in the hot strong coffee, with the Jamaica rum, and when all of your balls have been removed, add this to the skillet. Cook for a few minutes, stirring up all browned meat particles from bottom of skillet. Stir in the cream, and return the meat balls, together with the one cup diced pawpaw. Cover cooking container and simmer for about 15 minutes over lowest heat, turning balls once or twice with slotted spoon. Correct seasoning if necessary with a bit of salt, and serve while very hot, garnished on each portion with uncooked ripe pawpaw slices.

jamaica rum - beef stew
serves 4 to 6

Jamaica produces some very good beef and I take great pleasure in serving it at the table. Some times a judicious application of a little commercial meat tenderiser may be necessary, or marinating of the beef in moistened fresh pawpaw (papaya) leaves. These both produce very tender meat and still retain all of the beefy qualities which are so delightful to the palate.

Here is a special kind of Jamaican Beef Stew, which I heartily recommend to everyone. I like this with mashed yampies, well buttered and sprinkled with freshly-ground black pepper or whipped Irish potatoes, to which I like to add a touch of rich cream either fresh or from a tin. A light salad with tossed crisp lettuce and cucumber with suitable dressing, is a fine accompaniment. Also very acceptable is a loaf of crusty bread which has been thinly sliced, buttered and sprinkled with a touch of minced fresh parsley or fresh celery leaves wrapped loosely in aluminium foil and heated in an oven. One of the good imported wines especially a red wine such as Chateauneuf du Pâpe or Beaujolais, is almost obligatory.

2 tablespoons dark, or 3 tablespoons light, Jamaica rum
2 lbs lean beef, cut into neat 1 inch cubes
½ cup of flour
1 tablespoon salt
1 teaspoon freshly-ground black pepper
3 to 4 tablespoons cooking oil
1 large clove garlic, minced or mashed
2½ cups coarsely-chopped onion
2 cups coarsely-chopped sweet green pepper
6 scallions, with green tops, coarsely-chopped
1 large bay leaf
2 tablespoons Pickapeppa sauce
2 to 4 drops hot pepper sauce
3 tablespoons tomato paste, blended with
1 cup of water
2 teaspoons sugar
1½ cups peeled ripe tomatoes, cut into thin wedges
8 to 12 stuffed olives, thinly-sliced

Combine the flour, salt and black pepper in a firm bag shaking to mix. Dredge the beef cubes in this mixture, then brown the beef cubes in a large heavy skillet with cover. Cook a few at a time, in the oil until very well browned on all sides. Remove beef cubes as they are done and keep them warm in a covered container on lowest heat. When all of the meat is cooked add the garlic, onion, and sweet green pepper to the skillet. Cook, stirring often, until vegetables are just tender. Add the chopped scallions, reduce the heat, add the bay leaf, Pickapeppa and hot pepper sauces, tomato paste which has been thoroughly blended into the water and the sugar. Mix well, stirring up all bits of browned meat off the bottom of the pan, cover and simmer for about fifteen minutes stirring occasionally. Return the browned beef cubes, mix well, re-cover and simmer over lowest heat until the meat is tender. Add the rum, small wedges of ripe tomato, sliced stuffed olives, re-cover again and simmer for about ten minutes but no longer ! Season and serve in a large bowl from which each person helps himself.

glazed ham au rhum

For an extra festive touch to Baked Ham, consider this exceptional recipe which comes from the makers of Myers Rum.

2 tablespoons of Myers Rum
1 half ham (ready to eat type)
1 teaspoon dry mustard
3 tablespoons orange marmalade
cloves
maraschino cherry for garnish

Prepare the half ham for baking by cutting off the rind and excess fat. Make a paste of the mustard, marmalade and rum. Using a shaker bottle, moisten ham all over with Myers Rum, then spread the marmalade paste over the fat side of the ham. Slash the fat in either a diamond or squared pattern and stick with cloves in each diamond or square. Bake ham at 325°F for about one hour or for ten minutes per pound weight. During the last fifteen minutes, stick a maraschino cherry over each clove for garnish.

pork chops appleton serves 4

Pork in all of its forms takes very well to our special Jamaica rums. Here is one of my favourite ways of preparing good lean pork chops, in a refreshing sauce, to be served ideally in individual casseroles or ramekins, perhaps with hot fluffy rice and a big cabbage slaw as accompaniments.

2 jiggers light or dark Jamaica rum
8 lean pork chops, cut about ½-inch thick
2 tablespoons butter
½ cup finely-chopped onion
¼ cup finely-chopped sweet green pepper
¼ cup finely-chopped ripe tomato
¼ cup coarsely-chopped fresh ripe pineapple, or drained tinned chunks
salt and black pepper to taste

In a heavy skillet with cover, brown the chops on both sides in the butter, turning with kitchen tongs. Remove chops and keep them warm. Put the onion, green pepper, tomato, and pineapple, in the skillet, mix with the butter, and simmer, covered, for about 15 minutes, stirring occasionally. Return the pork chops, season to taste, re-cover the skillet and simmer the meat in the thick vegetable mixture until tender. Warm the Jamaica rum, pour over the pork chops, and flame. When the flames die down, serve chops and vegetable mixture, if desired in pre-heated individual casseroles or ramekins.

pork port royal serves 4

Pork and Jamaica rum are extremely compatible flavours. Here is one of my favourites, which I serve with hot fluffy rice, a salad of shredded cabbage, with a light dressing, and hot or iced tea. This Pork Port Royal is a lovely concoction, and one which I am certain will quickly become popular in your home.

2 tablespoons dark Jamaica rum
1 ½ lbs cubed lean pork
¼ cup light cooking oil
½ teaspoon salt
¼ teaspoon freshly-ground black pepper
4 tablespoons brown sugar
⅓ cup cider vinegar or more
2 tablespoons tomato ketchup
3 tablespoons soy sauce
2 tablespoons cornstarch (cornflour)
2 medium onions, peeled, halved, made into shells
2 or 3 small green peppers, cut into chunks
1 cup drained canned pineapple chunks
2 medium semi-ripe tomatoes, cut into wedges

Parboil the pork cubes in a little unsalted water for 10 minutes, and drain thoroughly. Pat pork cubes dry with paper towels. Put the oil in a large skillet with cover and over high heat brown the pork cubes on all sides with the salt, and pepper. Remove pork cubes with slotted spoon, and drain, keeping them warm. Meanwhile, mix the rum, brown sugar, vinegar, ketchup, soy sauce, and cornstarch (this dissolved in a bit of the juice from the tinned pineapple) together. Put in a heavy saucepan and bring this mixture to the boil, stirring constantly, until it thickens and becomes clear. Return pork cubes to the skillet, together with onion shells, green pepper chunks and pineapple chunks and pour over the hot sauce. Mix through, cover, and cook over medium heat, stirring gently once or twice, for about 12 minutes. About 2 minutes before serving, stir in the tomato wedges, and re-cover the skillet. All vegetables should retain much of their original crisp texture. Serve while very hot, over or alongside hot rice.

avocado jamaican serves 4

Beautiful rich Avocadoes, often called Avocado Pears or simply Pears, though they are members of the laurel family are plentiful in Jamaica. When they are in season, they form a special course at my table, in the following very distinctive fashion. I offer this just prior to the principal meat course, with memorable results.

1 tablespoon dark, or 2 tablespoons light Jamaica rum
2 tablespoons butter
1½ teaspoons tomato ketchup
1 tablespoon warm water
1 tablespoon wine or malt vinegar
1 tablespoon Pickapeppa or Worcestershire sauce
¼ teaspoon salt
½ teaspoon dry (powdered) mustard
4 whole cloves
2 or more drops Tabasco (hot pepper) sauce
1 tablespoon granulated sugar
2 ripe avocadoes, cut into halves

Prepare a hot sauce by thoroughly combining all the ingredients, except the Jamaica rum and the avocado. The avocadoes should be chilled, and cut in half at the last moment, to avoid discolouration. Bring sauce to a slow boil in a heavy saucepan, stirring constantly. Reduce heat, cover the saucepan, and simmer over lowest heat for 15 to 20 minutes. If desired, remove whole cloves. Stir in the Jamaica rum, and re-heat but do not boil. Serve in centres of freshly halved ripe avocadoes, as a special course.

tortilla de amarillo serves 4 to 6

Here is one of my old favourite recipes from Cuban days. It is a marvellous tropical omelet touched with Jamaica rum. I used to and still do, serve this at breakfast, luncheon, and dinner accompanied by ham, pork, sausages, chicken, and even hamburgers. See what you think. Its name means 'yellow omelet'.

1 to 2 tablespoons Jamaica rum, light or dark
4 large medium-ripe bananas, peeled
4 tablespoons butter
6 large eggs, separated
6 tablespoons milk
½ teaspoon salt
minced green scallions top or parsley for garnish

Slice the bananas crosswise on the diagonal about ¼ inch thick. Using a rather large heavy ovenproof skillet, sauté the banana slices in butter turning several times, until nicely browned on both sides. Remove banana slices with a slotted spoon or spatula. Combine slightly beaten egg yolks with milk and salt, then fold in the egg whites which have been beaten stiff. Pour this mixture into the skillet and arrange banana slices attractively in it. Pour over the rum to taste, and cook over low heat until egg mixture has risen and set. Immediately place in a pre-heated oven at 325°F until the omelet is nicely browned on top. Sprinkle with scallion tops or parsley, and serve at table immediately, directly from the hot skillet.

black beans in rum
serves 6

Jamaica rum, especially the dark variety, has considerable affinity with black beans or turtle beans, as in the following exceptional recipe. You may wish to serve this tempting dish with ham or pork, hot rice and perhaps a Caesar salad.

2 ozs dark Jamaica rum
1 lb dried black beans
1½ cups coarsely-chopped onion
2 large cloves garlic, minced or mashed
3 large stalks celery, coarsely-chopped
1 medium carrot, scraped, coarsely-chopped
2 tablespoons salt
¼ teaspoon freshly-ground black pepper
2 small bay leaves
¼ teaspoon oregano
1 tablespoon minced fresh parsley
4 tablespoons butter
1 pint commercial sour cream, at room temperature

Pick over and rinse the beans, place them in a large pot, add water to cover, put the lid on and bring quickly to the boil. Remove from heat and allow to stand, covered, for one hour. Then add the onion, garlic, celery, carrot, salt, pepper, bay leaves, oregano, and parsley, and over medium heat, adding water as needed, cook, still covered, until beans are almost tender. Correct seasoning and remove bay leaves. Turn beans out into a casserole, add the butter and one ounce of the Jamaica rum, mixing thoroughly. Cover and bake in a pre-heated oven at 350°F until the beans are completely tender. Remove from the oven, mix in the second portion of rum and top each serving, while hot, with a good portion of sour cream.

lima beans devon house
serves 6

Devon House is a magnificent restored private home, in Upper St Andrew, near to the tourist hotel complex of New Kingston. Under the supervision of the Jamaica Government, particularly The Hon. Mr Edward Seaga, Minister of Finance and Planning, Devon House has, since its opening a few years ago, become a popular place for visitors. It is also popular with the locals, as well, who enjoy its varied shops and the appealing Port Royal Grog Shoppe, which purveys a wondrous array of Jamaica rum beverages, as well as a unique indigenous cuisine.

Here we have a vegetable dish which is very much in keeping with the ambience of Devon House. Lima beans in Jamaica are sometimes called butter beans, or even white beans.

2 jiggers dark Jamaica rum, or 1 jigger dark, 1 jigger light
1 pound dried lima beans
1½ cups coarsely-chopped onion
2 medium cloves garlic, minced or mashed
3 large stalks celery, coarsely-chopped
1 medium carrot, scraped, finely-chopped
2 tablespoons salt
2 medium bay leaves, crumbled
½ teaspoon freshly-ground black pepper
¼ teaspoon oregano
2 teaspoons minced fresh parsley
4 tablespoons butter
1 pint commercial sour cream, at room temperature
paprika

Wash and pick over the dried beans, then place them in a large pot with cover, and add enough water to cover the beans. Cover and over high heat bring to the boil. Boil for two minutes, remove from the heat, and allow to stand, covered, for one hour. Add the onion, garlic, celery, carrot, salt, bay leaves, black pepper oregano, and parsley, and over medium heat, adding water if necessary, cook, covered, until beans are almost tender. Turn the beans out into an ovenproof casserole, remove the bay leaves, add the butter, and one jigger of the rum, mixing thoroughly. Cover and bake in preheated 350°F oven until the beans are completely tender. Remove from oven, mix in the second jigger of rum, and top each hot serving with a good portion of sour cream, sprinkled with paprika.

Note: I suggest accompanying this superlative dish with thinly-sliced ripe tomatoes which have been marinated in a sprinkling of olive oil and wine vinegar, with a touch of salt and freshly-ground black pepper, and either pan-fried or broiled thick pork chops. Hot fluffy rice, buttered crusty bread or rolls, and a bottle of well-chilled rosé or dry red wine make perfect accessories. Dessert, for me, is typically a selection of good cheese and crisp crackers, followed by Blue Mountain coffee, and a dram of Jamaica's own Rumona Liqueur.

carrots in piquant rum sauce   serves 4

Appetising tiny carrots are almost always available in markets everywhere in these bountiful times. These are highly nutritious vegetables and should be prepared with exceptional care, since overcooking, or improper cooking, can ruin not only their flavour but also their unique texture. I find the following recipe a perfect accompaniment to our prized ackees and saltfish, seafood, poultry, or beef, whether hamburgers or steaks.

2 tablespoons dark, or 3 tablespoons light Jamaica rum
3 cups small carrots, scraped, cut into neat slivers
1 cup water
1 teaspoon salt
4 tablespoons butter
2 tablespoons minced fresh parsley

Prepare the carrots, the freshest and smallest available, by rinsing, then scraping and then cutting into uniform neat slivers a couple of inches long and ¼ inch thick. Using a heavy saucepan with tight-fitting lid, bring the water with the salt to the boil, then plunge in the carrot slivers, re-cover, and cook for about ten minutes. Check if cooked. The carrots should still be rather crisp but not hard. Remove cover and cook, shaking the pan constantly over rather high heat, until almost dry. Add the Jamaica rum and the butter, reduce heat to medium degree, and simmer, covered again, until carrots are just tender. Correct seasoning with a tiny pinch of salt, and if desired a bit of freshly-ground black pepper. Serve while hot, sprinkled with fresh parsley. Be careful that this recipe does not scorch towards the end of its cooking.

stuffed sweet peppers runaway bay   serves 4

As a devoted fan of Jamaican food, I am always intrigued and delighted by the fresh vegetables on sale in our markets. In most other parts of the world, sweet peppers, or green or bell peppers as they are sometimes known are sizeable affairs. They can be four or five inches in vertical length, and sometimes are coarse textured. Here in the Caribbean, though, these crisp and tasty Capsicums are often smaller than one's fist, and lend themselves to stuffing, as in the following exciting recipe.

This is a main course entrée, which I like to serve for luncheon or a light supper, with heated crusty bread or toasted Jamaica bammy (cassava) wafers, and a beverage such as iced Blue Mountain coffee. Dessert is usually a selection of fresh fruit of the season, nicely arranged and well chilled.

1 tablespoon dark Jamaica rum
8 small sweet green peppers
2 tablespoons butter
⅓ cup finely-chopped scallions, with green tops
1 cup diced cooked chicken
½ cup diced cooked shrimp
4 tablespoons coarsely-chopped salted peanuts
2 cups freshly cooked rice
salt and freshly-ground black pepper

Neatly cut off tops of peppers and carefully scoop out the seeds and pithy ribs. Plunge peppers into boiling, lightly salted water and parboil for 3 minutes. Drain upside down. In a large skillet, melt butter and sauté scallions. Stir often and cook until soft but not browned. Add Jamaica rum, chicken, shrimp, peanuts, rice, salt and pepper to taste. Mix gently but well with a wooden spoon. Stuff the pepper shells with this mixture and set them upright in an ovenproof baking dish. Add enough water to bring the level up about an inch on the peppers. Bake in a pre-heated oven at 350°F for 20 minutes, basting with a small amount of water once. If desired, garnish with shrimp pieces and scallion tops. Serve two stuffed peppers, while hot, to each person.

sweet potato pudding liguanea   serves 4 to 6

Here in Jamaica, as almost everywhere else these days, Sweet Potatoes of top calibre are always available. With these and ripe bananas, allspice (pimento), and of course special Jamaica rum, I prepare the following pudding, which is one of the most popular dishes which I serve to my friends. This is a diversified creation. When hot it is a perfect accompaniment to almost any entrée as a vegetable. And then, if there are any leftovers, chill these thoroughly. Then slice them into thin pieces, with little cubes of cream cheese, perhaps finely chopped maraschino cherries, and if the occasion warrants, a warmed sauce of shredded coconut in a heavy sugar syrup. This makes an exotic dessert.

1 or 2 tablespoons Jamaica rum, light or dark
2 cups mashed cooked sweet potatoes
1 ⅓ cups mashed ripe bananas
1 cup milk
1 or 2 tablespoons granulated sugar
½ teaspoon salt
⅛ teaspoon ground allspice (pimento)
⅛ teaspoon grated nutmeg
2 egg yolks, beaten well
3 tablespoons chopped seedless raisins

In a large bowl, thoroughly blend the rum with the mashed sweet potatoes and bananas. Gradually add the milk, and mix until smooth. Add all the other ingredients, and mix thoroughly. Turn mixture into a well-buttered one-quart ovenproof casserole. Bake in preheated oven at 300°F for about 50 minutes, or until pudding is well set and firm and top is golden-brown in colour.

miss maude's fritters serves 6 or more

My good friend, Miss Maude Drum, is very fond of an occasional tot of Jamaica rum, but really prefers to use it in her ingenious cookery. These different and delicious fritters from Miss Maude's kitchen are served hot with beer or cocktails, or sprinkled with confectioner's (icing) sugar as dessert.

1 tablespoon light or dark Jamaica rum
2 cups cooked, mashed sweet potatoes
1 cup mashed ripe banana
1 cup canned crushed pineapple, drained
2 eggs, beaten lightly
¼ cup melted butter
½ teaspoon salt
1 cup flour
1 teaspoon baking powder
oil for deep frying
confectioners' (icing) sugar (optional)

Thoroughly combine the mashed sweet potatoes, banana and crushed pineapple with the eggs, melted butter and salt. Blend in the Jamaica rum. Sift in flour mixed with baking powder and mix thoroughly. Drop by small spoonfuls into deep oil heated to 375°F and cook until just golden in colour. Drain on absorbent paper towels and serve while very hot.

rummy turnips serves 4

Rum and turnips certainly sounds like a rather alien combination. But you will discover that it is perfectly delectable, and ideally suited to serve with such things as roast turkey or duck, and more than one of us hereabouts very much enjoy the side dish with roast beef, hamburgers and corned beef!

1 or 2 teaspoons light or dark Jamaica rum
1 lb small tender turnips
2 tablespoons butter
salt and freshly-ground black pepper to taste
½ cup heavy cream, whipped

Peel and quarter the turnips and cook, covered in boiling salted water until tender. Drain thoroughly and mash or put through potato ricer. Add butter, salt and pepper to taste, mix through, then fold in the whipped cream and Jamaica rum. Serve while hot.

jamaica coconut cream salad dressing serves 4 to 6

Here is a simple, delicious sauce for fruit salads, and one which is a great favourite. Use as wide a selection of fresh fruit as possible for your attractively presented salad, and, if desired, accompany with thinly-sliced baked or boiled ham and hot rolls as a light supper.

1½ cups coconut cream (see below), whipped
1 jigger light or dark Jamaica rum

Refer to the recipe for Rum Bullock, on page 21. Double the recipe, and allow prepared coconut milk to stand until a thicker liquid rises to the surface. This usually takes about an hour. Carefully remove this coconut cream and whip, adding the Jamaica rum, after chilling. Serve in a separate bowl with the fruit salad.

sweet potato camote
serves 6

In a number of tropical lands, from Mexico to the Philippines, one of the most popular desserts is a rather unusual creation made with sweet potatoes. In Jamaica, several of us enjoy this distinctive delight, called Camote, pronounced kah-*moe*-tay, made with our wonderful indigenous rums.

4 to 6 tablespoons light Jamaica rum

6 raw medium-size sweet potatoes, peeled

1 ½ cups dark brown sugar

¾ cup water

4 tablespoons butter

½ teaspoon salt

Cut the peeled sweet potatoes into quarters lengthwise. In a heavy saucepan, combine the sugar, water, butter, and salt and bring to the boil, stirring often. Add the pieces of sweet potato, adjust heat so the liquid just barely simmers, cover the pot and cook until potatoes are tender. When the potatoes first start to become tender (test by piercing carefully with a knife point), stir in the Jamaica rum. Allow sweet potato pieces to cool in the special syrup, and arrange them on a rack to drain and dry. When dry, chill prior to serving as a distinctive dessert.

rum raisin sauce
makes about 1½ cups

This luscious and easy sauce is perfection with beef tongue, baked ham and roast pork.

3 tablespoons dark or light Jamaica rum

1 can beef gravy

½ cup raisins

2 tablespoons minced onion

2 tablespoons currant jelly

1 tablespoon wine or cider vinegar

½ bay leaf, crumbled

1 teaspoon freshly-ground black pepper

Combine all ingredients in a heavy saucepan, and simmer for about 10 to 15 minutes, stirring often. Serve over sliced smoked tongue, baked ham, or roast pork. Heat slices of leftover meat in the sauce.

rum hard sauce

An appetising Rum Hard Sauce to be served on top of puddings such as Plum Pudding or Christmas Pudding and is an absolutely essential part of all good menus!

1 to 3 tablespoons light or dark Jamaica rum

2 tablespoons butter

1 cup sifted confectioner's sugar

Cream the butter until smooth and fluffy, using electric blender or beater if possible. Beat in the sugar until smooth, slowly add Jamaica rum to taste, and continue beating until very smooth. Chill and serve after cutting into small squares or other shapes, over hot puddings of many sorts.

avocado rum relish

Jamaica produces some exceptionally savoury, meaty avocadoes, often called pears in the countryside. Rum and avocado may seem, at first glance, to be rather an odd combination, but I think that if you try this relish with your next chicken, pork or ham dinner, you will agree that it is delicious.

3 tablespoons or more light Jamaica rum
1 large, fully ripe avocado, peeled, neatly diced
fresh lime juice to taste

Marinate the neat avocado cubes in the rum, with lime juice to taste, at room temperature for about 30 minutes before serving. It can be drained or not, according to taste and is a distinctive relish with chicken, pork or ham in particular.

coconut rum conserve

The coconut palms which abound in most parts of Jamaica are synonymous with the tropics. Their large fruits are utilised extensively in our cookery, from appetisers and soups to desserts, and include this lovely conserve, which is served with tea or at breakfast for toast or pancakes.

1 tablespoon light Jamaica rum
3 cups grated coconut meat
grated zest (outermost peel) of 1 ripe lime
4 cups water
5 $\frac{1}{3}$ cups granulated sugar

Carefully remove brown skin from coconut prior to grating. In a large heavy saucepan, add grated coconut meat, grated lime zest, and water. Heat to the boil, then add the sugar, mix through, and heat again to the boil. Lower heat and simmer gently for about an hour, or until syrup thickens to 220°F on a candy thermometer. Remove from heat, stir in Jamaica rum, and allow to cool before serving.

aunt anne's rum-coffee jelly   serves 4 to 6

My Aunt Anne was a formidable lady whose prime interests were making money, raising a motley assortment of stray cats, and eating and drinking very well indeed. One of her favourite refreshing courses after a big roast of beef, lamb or pork was this special chilled gelatin mixture. She also served it as a sort of preliminary dessert, invariably followed by cheese and fresh fruit.

1 tablespoon light or dark Jamaica rum
2 envelopes unflavoured gelatin
1 $\frac{1}{4}$ cups cold water
1 cup boiling water
$\frac{1}{2}$ cup granulated sugar
2 cups hot black strong coffee
1 cup whipped cream

In a large bowl mix together the gelatin and cold water, then add the boiling water. Mix until the gelatin is thoroughly dissolved. Stir in the Jamaica rum. Pour into attractive individual moulds and chill until very firm. Unmould and top each portion with whipped cream.

candied grapefruit peel
makes about ¾ pound

Candied citrus peels are exceptionally popular with everyone, and here is a special way to prepare grapefruit peel. Though most often made during the Christmas season, this confection is refreshing at all times of the year and keeps well in tightly covered jars.

1 tablespoon light Jamaica rum
peel from 2 large ripe grapefruit
water
½ teaspoon salt
¼ cup granulated sugar
½ cup honey, logwood if available
additional granulated sugar

Cover scrubbed peel with water and add the salt. Simmer in a large saucepan for 30 minutes. Drain, then cover with water and simmer until just tender. Drain again. Carefully remove all white inner part from peel and cut the remaining yellow peel into neat strips about 1 ½ inches long and ¼ inch wide, or a little larger, if desired. Bring the sugar, honey, and ¼ cup water to the boil in a heavy saucepan. Add the grapefruit peel and simmer until clear. Stir in Jamaica rum and allow peel to steep while cooling overnight. Re-heat peel and syrup next day, then drain, roll in additional granulated sugar, and arrange on waxed paper to dry. Store in neat layers in tight-covered jars.

rummed plums
makes 2 quarts

When fresh plums are in season, consider using some of them in rum preserves.

1 bottle (⅘ quart) light or white Jamaica rum
2 lbs fresh plums
2 lbs granulated sugar
4 thick slices lemon

Rinse and dry plums. Divide plums, sugar and lemon slices between 2 sterilised, wide-mouthed quart jars. Add Jamaica rum to fill each jar. Cover and allow to stand for at least 3 months and then serve as a special condiment.

chocolate rum fudge
makes about 1¾ lbs

For the sweet tooth, here is an exceptionally simple rich fudge, delicately flavoured with Jamaica rum.

1 tablespoon dark Jamaica rum
3 cups (three 6-ounce packages) semi-sweet chocolate chips
1⅓ cups canned sweetened condensed milk
pinch of salt
½ teaspoon vanilla extract
½ cup ground nuts

In top of a double boiler, melt chocolate over hot water, stirring occasionally. Remove from heat. Add the rum, condensed milk, salt, vanilla and ground nuts. Stir until smooth. Turn out into an 8-inch square pan neatly lined with waxed paper. Spread the mixture evenly and smooth the surface with a rubber spatula. Chill until firm. This normally takes about two hours. Turn out on to a cutting board, carefully peel off the paper and, with a sharp knife, cut into neat pieces. Store in an airtight container.

orange-rum blops

One of my favourite festive confections is the following one. It has subtle overtones of both oranges and Jamaica rum, all in a wonderful crunchy-nut mixture. They have always been called 'blops' by my family, for some nebulous reason, so 'blops' they remain.

1 tablespoon dark Jamaica rum
2½ cups granulated sugar
½ cup light brown sugar
1½ cups hot milk
¼ teaspoon salt
¼ lb butter, cut into small pieces
1 cup chopped walnuts, pecans, cashews or peanuts
1 tablespoon finely-grated orange zest

Place the cup of granulated and ½ cup of light brown sugar in a heavy saucepan. Over a medium heat, stirring constantly, melt the sugar until it becomes glossy. This usually takes about 10 minutes. Again stirring constantly, add the hot milk, salt and the 2 remaining cups of granulated sugar. Stir until this sugar dissolves completely. Boil without stirring until drops put into water form soft balls. This occurs when the candy thermometer reads about 236°F. A considerable amount of boiling is needed. Remove from the heat and blend in the Jamaica rum, butter, chopped nuts and grated orange zest. Allow to come to room temperature, then beat until creamy and drop in small dollops on to a greased cookie sheet or greased shallow pan. Store in tight-lidded containers.

rum balls
makes about 2 dozen

Ordinarily, these Rum Balls are served in most homes only around the Christmas season. But I see no reason whatsoever why they should not be offered to friends at any other time of the year! They also freeze very well.

2 tablespoons dark Jamaica rum
2 tablespoons butter, softened
1 egg yolk, beaten
¼ cup sifted confectioners' (icing) sugar
1 4-oz bar sweet cooking chocolate, finely-grated
chocolate cake sprinkles

Cream the butter until light and fluffy. Blend in the beaten egg yolk and gradually beat in the sugar. Beat in the Jamaica rum and the grated chocolate and beat until the mixture is smooth. Shape into neat balls about ½-inch in diameter. Roll them in chocolate cake sprinkles, coating them evenly, and place on waxed paper to chill very thoroughly.

coconut lace wafers

These crisp and rather fragile cookies must be stored in a tightly-lidded jar, assuming of course, that there are any left after the baking session!

2 tablespoons light Jamaica rum

¼ cup freshly-grated coconut

½ cup unsifted cake flour

¼ teaspoon double-acting baking powder

⅛ teaspoon baking soda

¼ cup granulated sugar

¼ cup light molasses

¼ cup butter

Mix flour, baking powder and soda. Combine sugar, molasses, and butter in a saucepan, and bring this to a full boil stirring all the time and cook for 1 minute. Remove from the heat, stir in the rum, then add the flour mixture and the coconut and mix well. Drop by ½ teaspoonfuls on to a lightly greased baking sheet. Bake only about 9 at a time, for ease in handling the wafers. Bake at 350°F. for 5 to 8 minutes. Cool slightly, then remove very carefully from the baking sheet, using a thin knife or a spatula. If wafer hardens on the baking sheet, return to the oven for a few minutes. If desired, while still warm, roll the wafers quickly over the handle of a wooden spoon to make tubes or cornucopias. Place on rack to cool and store in tight-lidded jars.

orange-rum brownies makes about 16

These chewy Brownies will be firm favourites with guests and every member of the family!

1 tablespoon dark or light Jamaica rum

3 tablespoons Fry's Cocoa

2 tablespoons finely-slivered orange rind

¼ cup water

1 cup sifted flour

¾ cup granulated sugar

2 large eggs, lightly beaten

½ teaspoon vanilla extract

½ cup margarine, melted

½ cup chopped nuts

Pre-heat oven to 350°F. Grease an 8-inch-square baking pan. Put tiny slivers of orange rind (with no white underpart) in the water in a small saucepan and bring to the boil. Reduce heat and simmer for 3 or 4 minutes. Drain thoroughly and cut strips into tiny pieces. Thoroughly combine all listed ingredients, adding the rum with the vanilla and turn into baking pan. Bake for about 20 minutes or test before if brownies are cooked. Allow to cool for at least 2 hours, then cut into neat squares.

coconut-rum cookies

The Coconut-Rum Cookies described below are easy to prepare and quickly disappear after they are cooked! If you have any left, store them in jars with tight-fitting lids.

½ jigger dark Jamaica rum

3½ cups shredded coconut

1 large tin sweetened condensed milk

Gently, but thoroughly combine all ingredients in a bowl. On a well-buttered baking sheet, pile mounded tablespoons of mixture about 1½ inches apart. Bake in a pre-heated oven at 375°F until the coconut begins to toast on top, usually about 25 minutes.

tropical moth balls

I wonder how these splendid goodies have received the name of Moth Balls! This is what they are called, however, and they are recommended for all, from Lepidopterists to Jamaica rum connoisseurs.

1 tablespoon dark Jamaica rum
1 cup softened butter
2 cups all-purpose flour
$\frac{1}{4}$ teaspoon finely-grated lime zest
4 tablespoons granulated sugar
1 $\frac{1}{2}$ cups coarsely-chopped cashews
1 cup confectioners' (powdered) sugar
1 cup lightly toasted grated coconut

Thoroughly cream the rum with the butter, flour, and lime zest in a bowl. Then, blend in the granulated sugar and nuts and mix well. Form the mixture into balls about $\frac{3}{4}$ inch in diameter. Bake these on an ungreased baking sheet in a pre-heated oven at 250°F for 30 minutes, then remove carefully with a spatula. Roll moth balls first in confectioners' sugar, then in the coconut. Allow to cool, and serve or store when well cooled in a tight-lidded jar.

st. mary orange rum cookies makes a considerable number

I am a great fan of cookies, in all of their varieties, shapes and sizes. I delight in offering my friends the following unique version, which I developed some time ago and of which I am rather proud. I have named these to honour one of my favourite Jamaican parishes, where all of the ingredients abound.

4 teaspoons light Jamaica rum
$\frac{1}{2}$ cup softened butter
$\frac{3}{4}$ cup brown sugar (light variety, if possible)
1 large fresh egg
$\frac{1}{2}$ teaspoon grated orange rind
1 teaspoon fresh orange juice
1 $\frac{1}{2}$ cups sifted all-purpose flour
$\frac{1}{2}$ teaspoon baking powder
$\frac{1}{8}$ teaspoon salt
pinch ground allspice

In a large bowl, cream together the softened butter and the brown sugar. Add the egg and beat with fork until very light and fluffy. Add the Jamaica rum, plus all the other ingredients and mix until very thoroughly blended. Drop by level teaspoonfuls on to an ungreased baking sheet. Press very flat and bake in a pre-heated oven at 375°F for about 7 minutes. Remove from the oven and allow to cool for a minute or so, then carefully remove the cookies with a spatula and cool on kitchen towels. Store in a tightly-lidded large jar, to retain crispness, which is most desirable.

fat rum cookies
makes about 48 cookies

Everyone likes cookies and I have found that these fat rum cookies are favourites with everyone acquainted with the easy recipe. They are lovely warm from the oven and I think they are even better if allowed to mellow, stored in tight-lidded containers.

2 teaspoons dark Jamaica rum

½ cup softened butter

1 cup firmly-packed brown sugar

2 eggs

2 cups sifted cake flour

1 teaspoon baking powder

½ teaspoon salt

1 teaspoon ground cinnamon

¼ teaspoon ground cloves

¼ teaspoon ground nutmeg

2 cups seeded or seedless raisins, chopped

½ cup chopped peanuts, cashews or other nuts

Cream together the rum, butter and brown sugar. Add the eggs, one at a time, beating until the mixture is fluffy, after each addition. Add flour, salt, cinnamon, cloves and nutmeg sifted together. Then add the raisins and the nuts of your choice. Mix well. Drop by teaspoonfuls on to a greased cookie sheet, allowing room for considerable spreading. Bake in a pre-heated oven at 350°F for about 10 minutes. Do not overbake!

jamaica coconut custard pie

This special version of a coconut custard pie is very tropical and appetising.

2 tablespoons light Jamaica rum

unbaked 9-inch pastry shell

⅔ cup canned sweetened condensed milk

2 cups hot water

¼ teaspoon salt

½ teaspoon vanilla extract

3 large fresh eggs

1 cup grated coconut

¼ cup toasted grated coconut

nutmeg

In a medium bowl, blend together sweetened condensed milk, water, salt, rum, and vanilla extract. In a small bowl, beat eggs until just blended. Stir into condensed milk mixture, together with the 1 cup of grated coconut. Pour into the pastry shell and sprinkle with a dash of nutmeg. Bake in a pre-heated oven at 425°F for 10 minutes. Reduce heat to 300°F and bake for 20 to 25 minutes or until a knife inserted in the centre comes out clean. Allow to cool at room temperature, then chill and serve sprinkled with toasted coconut.

chocolate rum pie

Mrs Amy O'Brien of Kingston makes ornamental candles and, as well as being a talented craftswoman, she is also a talented cook. Here is her special recipe for Chocolate Rum Pie.

¼ cup light or dark Jamaica rum
¾ cup granulated sugar
1 envelope unflavoured gelatin
dash salt
1 cup milk
2 beaten egg yolks
1 6-oz package semi-sweet chocolate pieces, or 1 cup
2 egg whites
1 cup heavy whipping cream
1 teaspoon vanilla extract
1 baked 9-in. pie shell, preferably made from crushed graham crackers
heavy cream, whipped
pecan halves or pieces

In a heavy saucepan, combine ½ cup of the sugar, gelatin and salt. Stir in milk and egg yolks. Cook and stir over a low heat until slightly thickened. Remove from heat, add chocolate pieces and stir until melted. Add the rum. Chill until partially set. Beat egg whites until soft peaks form. Gradually add the other ¼ cup of sugar and beat until stiff peaks form. Fold into the chocolate mixture. Whip the cream with the vanilla. Layer the whipped cream and chocolate mixture into the pastry shell, ending with whipped cream. Save a little cream for decoration. Swirl the top to marble and chill until firm. Decorate on top with the additional whipped cream and pecans and serve well chilled.

cream cheese and rum pie

This is a sort of cream cheese pie, subtly flavoured with Jamaica rum, and has proved exceptionally popular.

1½ teaspoons dark Jamaica rum
⅛ lb butter
18 graham crackers
3 small packages cream cheese
2 eggs, beaten
1 teaspoon or more cream
½ cup granulated sugar
1 pint commercial sour cream
5 tablespoons granulated sugar
pinch ground cinnamon

Prepare the crust by melting the butter, then add the thoroughly crushed graham crackers and mix well. Line a pie plate with this mixture and bake crust in a pre-heated oven at 370°F for 5 minutes. Prepare the filling by beating together the softened cream cheese, cream and half cup of granulated sugar until smooth adding a little more cream if needed. Beat in the eggs and one teaspoon dark Jamaica rum. Fill the pie crust and bake for 20 minutes. Meanwhile, blend the 5 tablespoons of granulated sugar, cinnamon, and the other half teaspoon Jamaica rum to the sour cream. Spread this over the pie, return to the oven and bake for 5 minutes. Cool the pie, then chill very thoroughly and serve.

drunken cake (panetela borracha)   serves about 12

Drunken cake is the translation of panetela borracha. This is a favourite dessert throughout parts of tropical America and has various versions. Here is my special recipe, which I like to serve with thin slices of ripe mango or paw-paw.

1 cup light Jamaica rum
angel food cake, or pound cake, cut into neat 2-in squares
2 cups water
4 cups granulated sugar
½ teaspoon ground cinnamon
½ teaspoon ground allspice (pimento)
juice and grated rind of 1 ripe lime
2 teaspoons vanilla extract
rum-flavoured whipped cream
thin slices of ripe fresh or tinned mango or paw-paw (optional, but nice)

In a heavy saucepan, combine the water, sugar, cinnamon, allspice, strained lime juice and grated lime rind and bring to the boil. Boil, stirring occasionally with wooden spoon, for 5 minutes. Lower heat, add vanilla extract and allow to cool. Stir in the Jamaica rum. Pour over individual squares of cake, and top with lightly rum-flavoured whipped cream, garnished if desired with a couple of slices of mango or pawpaw. Serve chilled or at room temperature.

jamaican trifle serves about 8

Just about every cook in this part of the world has her or his special recipe for a trifle, a heritage from when the British ruled Jamaica. This recipe for a Jamaican trifle is for a special trifle with a unique flavour.

about ½ cup light or dark Jamaican rum
2 egg yolks
2 tablespoons sugar
1 cup scalded milk
2 layers of plain sponge cake
strawberry or raspberry jam
2 ripe bananas, thinly sliced lengthwise
½ cup or more coarsely-broken cashews
1 cup heavy cream, whipped
candied cherries, angelica, and chopped pistachios

Prepare soft custard by placing egg yolks, sugar and cup of scalded milk in top of a double boiler over hot water. Cook, stirring often, until thickened. Allow to cool, and blend in about 1 teaspoon of the rum and chill. Arrange one of the sponge cake layers in a glass serving dish. Spread liberally with jam of your choice, top with long banana slices and sprinkle liberally with broken up cashews. Gently pour over part of rum to soak the cake, but do not make it mushy. Top with the soft custard and place the second sponge cake layer on top of the custard. Spread with jam, dredge with the remaining Jamaica rum and top with whipped cream. Garnish attractively with candied cherries, pieces of angelica and coarsely-chopped pistachio nuts. Chill thoroughly and serve.

banana-marmalade fool
serves 6

There are a lot of different kinds of Fools in the culinary world, the puréed fruit combination with various sorts of cream or custard mixtures and few of them are as appealing as this one from Jamaica.

2 tablespoons light Jamaica rum

3 tablespoons tart orange marmalade

2 cups mashed ripe bananas

3 egg yolks, beaten

¼ cup heavy cream, whipped

3 egg whites, beaten

2 tablespoons confectioners' sugar

pinch freshly-grated nutmeg

Beat the egg yolks in a large bowl until they thicken. Then blend in the mashed bananas, orange marmalade and Jamaica rum, mixing very thoroughly. Pour into parfait glasses and chill. Prior to serving, whip cream and add some to each glass. Whip the egg whites with sugar and top off each glass with this sprinkling each portion with nutmeg. Serve at once.

rum orange slices   serves 4

Oranges, perhaps more than all other sorts of citrus fruits are good accompaniments to Jamaica rum. Here, for instance, is an exceptional dessert using Navel or Temple oranges, if possible.

light or dark Jamaica rum

2 large sweet oranges

granulated sugar to taste

about 2 tablespoons butter

Carefully peel the oranges, remove all the white pith. With a sharp knife, cut into neat slices about ¼-inch thick, discarding any seeds that may be present. Arrange in an ovenproof glass pie plate or shallow baking dish, overlapping slices as little as possible. Sprinkle with light or dark Jamaica rum to taste, then sprinkle with granulated sugar and dot evenly with butter. Allow to stand for about 15 minutes. Just before serving, run the container under a preheated grill until the butter bubbles and the topping has lightly browned. Serve without delay, removing slices carefully with a spatula and pour over equal amounts of Jamaica rum.

rummy watermelon

A distinctive and tasty method of serving a very ripe Watermelon is the following one.

Jamaica rum, light or dark

watermelon

Using a sharp, small knife, cut a 3-inch square plug from the melon and put this on one side. Pour Jamaica rum into the hole, a little at a time, until no more will be absorbed. Fit the plug back in place and seal the edges with masking tape. Refrigerate melon for at least 12 hours, then cut into neat wedges, unpeeled, and serve.

hot and cold jamaica rum dessert   serves 6

Making use of several readily available ingredients, one can create, in a hurry, the following exciting dessert. It is refreshing and is counted amongst my personal favourites in the rum dessert category.

2 tablespoons light Jamaica rum
¼ cup butter
½ cup firmly-packed light brown sugar
2 teaspoons fresh lime juice
6 slices fresh or tinned pineapple
3 ripe bananas
vanilla ice cream

Melt the butter in a small heavy saucepan and then add the brown sugar. Heat, stirring constantly, until this is dissolved. Stir in the Jamaica rum and lime juice and simmer for a moment, still stirring. Place pineapple slices in a shallow individual baking dish or ramekin. Pour half of the sauce over these slices and bake in a pre-heated oven at 400°F for 10 minutes, turning once. Peal ripe bananas, cut lengthwise and across to make four pieces out of each banana. Set two pieces of banana on each pineapple slice, and pour over remaining sauce. Return to the oven for 5 to 7 additional minutes. Remove and top liberally with ice cream and serve immediately.

rum pot   serves 8

Rum pots have long been popular in many parts of the world, the varied fruits being slowly marinated in large stoneware crocks in a cool cellar. Here is a modernised version of this traditional delight, and one that retains all the old-fashioned goodness.

½ cup dark Jamaica rum
1 lb can pear halves
1 lb can peach halves
1 lb can pineapple chunks
¼ cup granulated sugar
3 whole cloves
2 whole allspice berries (pimento)
1 ½-in piece of fresh ginger-root, or ½ teaspoon ground ginger
1 cup fresh or frozen strawberries or raspberries
1 teaspoon lime or lemon juice

Drain the canned fruit, reserving ½ cup of the combined syrups. Heat the fruit syrup, sugar, whole cloves, allspice berries and ginger-root or ground ginger, in a heavy saucepan. When the mixture boils, remove from the heat and add all fruits and the lime or lemon juice. Cool, stir in the Jamaica rum, then chill thoroughly.

rum with fruit

Almost any fresh or tinned fruit can quickly and easily be made into a memorable dessert if flavoured with a little Jamaica rum, either light or dark, depending on your mood and on the menu preceding. Consider, for example, pineapple, guava, pawpaw (papaya), citrus in variety (a combination is delicious), peach, pear, apple, strawberry. A tropical fruit compote, perhaps with a touch of coconut, slivered cashews, peanuts or almonds. Do not add too much rum, though, or the flavour of the fruit or fruits might be overwhelmed! The rum should be used to give a special, subtle and different taste.

fig balls makes about 1½ pounds little balls

These Fig Balls originated in the Algarve, where they are very popular with coffee after dinner. My own version of these Bolas de Figo contains Jamaica rum and I think the results are something special!

1 jigger light or dark Jamaica rum
½ lb peeled, blanched almonds
½ lb dried figs
1 teaspoon grated orange zest
1 square baker's chocolate
½ lb granulated sugar
7 tablespoons water
additional granulated sugar

Lightly roast almonds on a baking sheet in a slow oven until nicely browned on all sides, shaking and turning them often to avoid scorching. Remove bits of stalk from the dried figs. Put almonds, figs, orange zest, and chocolate through fine grid of your food grinder, or whirl until well chopped in electric blender. The mixture should be rather coarse and not smooth. Boil together the sugar and water until thickened in a heavy saucepan. Remove from heat, stir in the Jamaica rum, together with ground ingredients, mixing well. When cool, form into balls about ½ inch in diameter, roll in additional granulated sugar, and serve chilled. Store in tight-covered jars.

apricot-rum parfaits

This attractive parfait of mashed tinned apricots is easy to make and should ideally be served accompanied by home-made nutty chocolate brownies!

3 tablespoons light or dark Jamaica rum
1 large can apricots, drained
3 egg whites
¼ cup heavy whipping cream

Force drained apricots through a sieve. Whip the egg whites until stiff, and whip the cream also until stiff, but separately. Blend the apricots and whipped cream gently together. Then fold in the egg whites gradually, together with the Jamaica rum. Chill thoroughly and serve cold in chilled parfait glasses.

apricots dorotea

I never know whether to call this creation a sweet salad or a semi-sweet dessert. But whatever its nomenclature, Apricots Dorotea have proved to be exceptionally popular. And who is Dorotea? Ah, that is my secret!

1 jigger light Jamaica rum
1 large can apricot halves, drained
1 pint cottage cheese
1 tablespoon minced maraschino cherries
½ cup heavy cream
1 teaspoon light Jamaica rum
curls of bitter or semi-sweet chocolate

Gently but thoroughly combine the cheese with a jigger of light rum and the minced cherries. Fill the cavities of the drained apricot halves and put each pair back together, to form a whole fruit with a median ring of red-flecked cottage cheese. Chill thoroughly, and serve topped with rum-flavoured whipped cream, sprinkled with curls of chocolate.

rum-soursop cream

One of the more unusual tropical fruits abounding in Jamaica is the Soursop. It is a large prickly green fruit, with a sweet, creamy flesh surrounding large, black seeds. Tinned soursop nectar, also known by its Spanish name of Guanâbana, is available overseas, and makes the following lovely dessert.

Jamaica rum, light or dark
1 ripe soursop or
tinned soursop nectar
nutmeg

If you are using a fresh soursop, peel it and force the flesh through a sieve. To either the fresh soursop or the tinned nectar, blend in the rum to taste. Chill in individual pots de crême. Serve very cold, and, if desired, add freshly-grated nutmeg.

tropical prune compote
serves 6

A hearty yet refreshing dessert is this Tropical Prune Compote, which can well be accompanied by thin crisp sugar cookies.

½ cup dark or punch Jamaica rum
1 lb large dried prunes
1 cup water
curl of ripe lime peel
¼ teaspoon ground allspice
pinch of ground cloves
shredded coconut, lightly toasted

In a saucepan with cover, place the rum, prunes, water, piece of lime peel, allspice, and ground cloves. Bring to the boil, then reduce heat and simmer, covered, until prunes are tender. Allow to cool, then chill, to serve with each portion sprinkled liberally with lightly toasted shredded coconut.

pineapple negril
serves 4 to 6

Some of the most spectacular white sand beaches are to be found at Jamaica's western tip, Negril. I would imagine that the following lovely dessert would taste even better eaten under the trees at Negril!

1 tablespoon or more dark Jamaica rum
1 large ripe pineapple, peeled and cored, cut into ½-in thick slices
3 tablespoons butter
coffee ice cream
minced green maraschino cherries
whipped cream flavoured with additional dark Jamaica rum

In a heavy skillet, sauté the pineapple slices in the butter until lightly browned on both sides, turning as needed. Towards end of cooking, sprinkle both sides with the dark Jamaica rum. Remove slices with a slotted spatula and allow to cool. To serve, top each slice with a good scoop or two of coffee ice cream. Blend the minced green maraschino cherries into the whipped cream which has been flavoured to taste with additional dark Jamaica rum, and top each portion with this.

peach compote   serves 6

In a few of our mountain gardens, small Ceylon peaches are raised each year. But most Jamaicans prefer their peaches from a tin, and these are really easier for this pleasant dessert compote.

2 tablespoons light or dark Jamaica rum
2 large cans peach halves
¼ cup light corn or cane syrup
⅛ teaspoon almond extract or essence
2 tablespoons honey

Drain peaches, and, in a heavy saucepan combine the syrup with the corn or cane syrup and the almond extract. Bring to the boil, and gently cook the peach halves, a couple at a time, until they are heated through. This usually takes about 2 minutes. Remove peach halves with slotted spoon, and arrange in individual large goblets, brandy snifters, or glass bowls. Boil syrup until very thick, add the honey and pour over peaches. Chill, and stir in Jamaica rum just prior to serving.

flaming rum omelet serves 4

One of the most spectacular of Jamaica rum desserts is a Flaming Rum Omelet. As with every good omelet, it must be prepared just before required and served on a piping hot platter or directly from the baking skillet, on to pre-heated individual plates! When done with attention to detail, this is a fantastic recipe. It can equally well form a light entrée for a late evening supper as well as a finale to the main menu.

1 tablespoon dark, or two tablespoons light Jamaica rum
6 large fresh eggs
1 teaspoon granulated sugar
4 teaspoons milk
2 tablespoons butter
Jamaica guava jelly
3 or 4 tablespoons light Jamaica rum

Use a large heavy skillet that can be placed in the oven. Separate the eggs and beat the yolks with the first listed Jamaica rum, sugar and milk. Beat the whites separately until they are stiff but not dry, and gently fold them into the beaten yolks. Meanwhile, melt the butter in the skillet. Add the egg mixture to this, and cook over a low heat on top of the stove for about 5 minutes. The omelet should be puffy and slightly brown on the bottom, test by gently turning up one corner with a spatula. Place in a pre-heated oven at 400° F to brown nicely on top, usually about 8 to 10 minutes. Arrange guava jelly around the edges of the omelet and serve directly from the skillet. If you prefer, transfer the omelet to a heated sizeable platter, adorn with guava jelly and warm the final Jamaica rum, pour over the omelet and flame at the table. When the flames die down, cut into liberal wedges, and serve, each portion receiving some of the melting guava jelly.

jamaica rum fondue
serves 4 to 6 liberally

Fondues are popular in this country and normally we think of Swiss Cheese Fondue or Beef Fondue Bourguignonne or Fondue Orientale with sea food. Each of these are accompanied by a variety of condiment dishes or dips, or as with the cheese fondue, just crusty good quality bread cubes.

But, by using a special set of long handled, long-tined Fondue forks, and a chafing dish or special Fondue apparatus, how about the following dessert Jamaica Rum Fondue?

Be sure that you arrange the dipping pieces of fruit and cake inventively and attractively on several plates. Use white unadorned plates to display the handsome colours and subtle textures of the ingredients. I like to garnish my serving plates with a few fresh tropical blossoms, rinsed and then refreshed for a while in a refrigerator. Be careful that your guests do not try to 'dunk' these, too, as did some of my recent happy guests!

With a marvellous largesse of tropical and imported fruits available in this country, your extra special Fondue should present at least four different fruits. A good firm pound cake or sponge cake is needed too, cut into inch broad cubes and toasted lightly in a pre-heated oven at 350°F. for just a few minutes, turning them a couple of times. Consider everything from banana, mango, pineapple and Otahiete apple and just ripe pawpaw (papaya) to apple, pear, peach, and grape. Also use star-apple, naseberry and guava!

4 tablespoons light or dark Jamaica rum
1 tablespoon butter
3 oz bars plain milk chocolate
1 cup heavy cream
1 cup milk
2 tablespoons granulated sugar

Using a chafing dish over hot water, or a special fondue pot, melt the butter and bars of chocolate together with the Jamaica rum, stirring often, until thoroughly blended. Gradually blend in the cream, milk, and sugar, stirring constantly until a smooth mixture is attained. Maintain over lowest flame and spear the suggested ingredients listed above on your fondue fork to cook briefly in the mixture. Serve immediately but warn about the hot forks!

crêpes carlos

One of the most elegant ways to use Jamaica rum as a dessert is in Crêpes Carlos. I believe that this recipe was invented by the late Helen Evans Brown. I do not know who Carlos was, but I am certain he is or was very proud of his namesake!

¼ cup of Jamaica rum, light or dark
prepared thin French crêpes
1 pineapple, fresh and very ripe
¼ cup of butter
apricot jam or preserves
6 tablespoons Jamaica rum (optional)

Prepare your favourite thin French crêpes. Cut the juicy flesh of the pineapple into neat chunks. Cook the pineapple pieces in the butter until lightly browned on both sides adding the rum towards the end of cooking. Spread the crêpes with the jam or preserves and fold each into quarters. Arrange in a large chafing dish placing them on one side. On the other side of the dish put the cooked pineapple pieces. Pour all the pan juices over the crêpes and heat gently. If desired, just before serving, add 6 more tablespoons of rum. Flame and serve.

dessert pancake with hard sauce

Tiny pancakes touched with Jamaica rum and grated lime zest, topped with hard sauce, form a distinctive and attractive dessert.

1 jigger light or dark Jamaica rum
1 tablespoon finely-grated lime zest (rind)
2 cups prepared pancake batter
rum hard sauce   see page 42

Prepare your favourite pancake batter, which should not be too thick, and blend in the jigger of Jamaica rum and the grated lime zest. Drop on to lightly greased hot griddle or skillet, by the teaspoonful, and bake until nicely browned on both sides. Serve hot, with Rum Hard Sauce.

cold rum-mocha soufflés
serves 4 to 6

A special delight at my house is an array of individual chilled Rum-Mocha Soufflés. These require a little extra labour on the part of the chef but the results are well worth it.

2 tablespoons dark Jamaica rum
4 large fresh eggs
4 tablespoons sugar
2 tablespoons powdered instant Blue Mountain coffee
½ pint heavy cream
2 tablespoons milk
grated bitter chocolate

Separate the eggs and beat the yolks with the sugar and powdered coffee until thick and creamy. Stir in the rum. Whip the cream, plus the whole milk and gently fold into the rum-mocha mixture. Beat the egg whites until stiff but not dry and gently fold these into the mixture. Turn into individual soufflé dishes or custard cups and place in the freezing compartment of your refrigerator for at least 2 hours. Serve direct from the refrigerator, each soufflé sprinkled with the grated chocolate.

banana quit parfait
serves 8 to 10

My culinary and horticultural colleague, Edward A. Flickinger, has come up with a superb frozen parfait dessert, which he has named after our Banana Quit birds.

⅓ cup Appleton Special rum
4 medium fully ripe bananas
⅓ cup brown sugar
2 tablespoons heavy cream
1 teaspoon ground cinnamon
¼ teaspoon ground Jamaica allspice (pimento)
1 teaspoon vanilla extract
½ gallon vanilla ice cream
½ pint heavy cream, whipped with sugar and vanilla to taste
maraschino cherries
freshly-grated nutmeg

Combine ingredients from Appleton Special rum to the vanilla extract together in an electric blender until all well blended. Into 8 to 10 parfait glasses or tall pilsner beer glasses, scoop alternative layers of ice cream and Jamaica rum sauce until nearly full. Top with whipped cream and cherry and the grated nutmeg to taste. Place the prepared parfaits in the refrigerator freezer compartment or in a deep freeze for at least one hour before serving.

chocolate-rum parfaits
serves 8

Parfaits are favoured desserts with many people and few which I serve at my Jamaican table have more general appeal than this elegant yet easy recipe.

6 tablespoons dark Jamaica rum

2 envelopes unflavoured gelatin

¼ cup cold milk

¾ cup milk, heated to the boiling point

1 egg

¼ cup granulated sugar

⅛ teaspoon salt

1 6-oz package (1 cup) semi-sweet chocolate pieces

2 cups heavy cream, divided

1½ cups crushed ice

1 teaspoon vanilla extract

½ cup chopped roasted pecans

Sprinkle gelatin over dark Jamaica rum and cold milk in an electric blender and allow to stand for a few minutes. Add boiling milk, and blend at low speed until gelatin dissolves, using rubber spatula to push all gelatin granules into mixture. Add egg, sugar, and salt. Turn control to high speed and add chocolate pieces. Blend until smooth, then add 1 cup heavy cream. Gradually add crushed ice, blending until mixture is smooth. Then allow to stand for 15 minutes, to thicken. Add vanilla to remaining 1 cup heavy cream, and whip until stiff. In chilled parfait glasses alternate chocolate mixture, whipped cream and chopped roasted pecans. Serve immediately or chill thoroughly and then serve, the latter preferred.

rum chocolate mousse
highgate   serves 4 to 6

Here is a Mousse which is uniquely Jamaican, yet justifiably popular in other countries, since the essential ingredients are widely available.

2 tablespoons dark Jamaica rum

6 ozs semi-sweet chocolate

1 tablespoon powdered instant Blue Mountain coffee

3 tablespoons butter

6 large eggs, separated

5 tablespoons granulated sugar

½ cup heavy cream

Using a double boiler, heat the chocolate with the coffee powder and the dark Jamaica rum, over hot but not boiling water until all has melted and blended together. Stir often. Add the butter and continue to stir until melted. Put the egg yolks in a bowl and beat until light. Add a small amount of the rum-chocolate-coffee mixture and with a fork or whisk beat until thoroughly blended. Then add the remainder of the rum-chocolate-coffee mixture, turn back into top of the double boiler, and beat, still over the hot water until smooth. Remove from heat and allow to cool. Whip the cream, and add the sugar gradually and thoroughly. Then beat egg whites until very stiff. Fold the whipped cream and egg whites into the rum-chocolate-coffee mixture thoroughly, turn into an attractive serving bowl, and chill until firm, ideally overnight to serve.

mincemeat mousse tower suite   serves 6

What a distinctive dessert this Jamaica rum-flavoured mousse is! It is one of the innumerable specialties of the Tower Suite restaurant in New York City, but a number of us here in Jamaica prepare it with pleasure on frequent occasions.

2 jiggers light or dark Jamaica rum

1 envelope unflavoured gelatin

2 tablespoons cold water

½ cup boiling water

4 egg yolks

½ cup granulated sugar

4 cups heavy cream

½ cup mincemeat, homemade or tinned, drained

Sprinkle gelatin over cold water in a bowl and allow to soften. Add boiling water, and stir until gelatin is dissolved. In another bowl, beat egg yolks thoroughly and gradually beat in sugar until mixture is thickened and creamy. Stir in the gelatin then fold in the heavy cream which has been whipped until it is firm but not at all stiff, the drained mincemeat and the Jamaica rum of your choice. Turn mixture in to a 6-cup mould and chill until set, usually about 2 hours. Unmould to serve.

rum sabayon   serves 6

Sabayon or zabaglione is a classic French or Italian dessert made with Marsala wine or sherry. But here in Jamaica, we use our lovely light rum, and serve our own version to special guests!

3 to 4 tablespoons light Jamaica rum

5 egg yolks

1 tablespoon cold water

¾ cup granulated sugar

⅛ teaspoon salt

In top of a double boiler, beat the egg yolks with water until they are foamy and light. Whisk in sugar, salt, and rum. Beat over hot, not boiling, water, until thickened and fluffy for a few minutes. Pile into sherbert glasses, and serve while hot.

ginger-rum ice cream

When you can acquire preserved stem ginger in syrup, use your good light Jamaica rum and prepare a batch of this marvellous ice cream!

1 jigger light Jamaica rum

½ cup preserved stem ginger

3 cups heavy cream

2 teaspoons lemon or lime juice

½ cup granulated sugar

2 tablespoons ginger syrup

2 tablespoons strained honey

Chop the stem ginger, very finely, and drain well. Thoroughly mix together all ingredients, and freeze either in electric or hand-cranked ice cream freezer, or in refrigerator trays, the former preferred for smoothness.

rum rice pudding
serves 4 to 6

I have long been inordinately fond of Rice Pudding, in all of its international variations. Try the following recipe presented icy-cold in an attractive serving dish, such as one utilised for making soufflés, directly from the refrigerator. I delight in offering thin crisp cookies, sprinkled prior to baking with finely-chopped almonds or peanuts, as a pleasant adjunct to this creation.

1 tablespoon dark, or 2 tablespoons light Jamaica rum
2½ cups freshly-cooked rice
¾ cup granulated sugar
¼ teaspoon vanilla extract
½ cup seedless or seeded raisins, plumped, drained
5 large fresh eggs, beaten
2 cups milk
⅛ teaspoon salt
⅓ cup grated coconut

In a large bowl, mix together the cooked rice, about half of the sugar, the vanilla extract, the raisins (these plumped for 10 minutes or so in a small amount of warm water, then drained thoroughly, and if desired cut into smallish pieces), and the Jamaica rum. In another bowl, beat the eggs, then add the milk, the remaining sugar, and the salt. Turn into a well-buttered baking dish, and bake in pre-heated oven at 350°F until the pudding has set, usually about 35 minutes. Sprinkle with grated coconut about 5 minutes before removing from oven, so that this topping browns nicely. Serve pudding either warm, or chill and offer portions with heavy whipped cream.

rumona delight

Rumona is a delightfully different Jamaican liqueur, and made from fine quality rum. You will find it is superb when spooned over your favourite ice cream and as an addition to dessert sauces, cake icings, puddings and soufflés, it is unique in its special category. Here is an exceptionally showy dessert, guaranteed to intrigue and please your guests.

coffee ice cream
vanilla ice cream
strong black coffee, ideally Jamaican
egg whites, whipped with sugar to taste
Rumona Liqueur
toasted chopped almonds

Pour into a tall, cold parfait glass a layer of chilled, strong black coffee, laced with Rumona. Add successive layers of vanilla ice cream, egg whites whipped with a little sugar until almost stiff but not dry, and finally a scoop of coffee ice cream. Sprinkle each serving with toasted chopped almonds and pour over the top a dash of Rumona and serve at once.

ice cream sodas with rum

The next time you prepare an ice cream soda at home, or maybe chocolate milk using canned chocolate syrup, add a good teaspoon or more of either light or dark Jamaica rum.

coffee spanish main
serves 6

This Coffee Spanish Main is one of the most extraordinary ways of serving our superb Blue Mountain Coffee that I have ever encountered. It comes to us through the courtesy of the Sheraton-Kingston Hotel.

6 ounces medium Jamaica rum (Appleton Special is recommended)

peel of ½ ripe Jamaica orange

1 good pinch freshly-grated nutmeg

1 stick cinnamon

6 pieces lump (cube) sugar

6 cups strong Blue Mountain Coffee

Finely grate orange rind. Let it soak in rum, along with grated nutmeg and the cinnamon stick, this broken up into smallish pieces if desired. When ready to serve, remove cinnamon pieces. Pour very hot coffee into goblets or demi-tasse coffee cups, which should be pre-rinsed with hot water. On top of each glass or cup, place coffee spoon with a lump (cube) of sugar in it. Soak each sugar lump with part of the rum mixture, and flame it. When sugar crumbles, let it sink into the glass or cup. Pour in remainder of rum mixture, in equal distribution and serve immediately.

cold buttered rum
serves 1

These days, fabulous Jamaica rums are utilised in a great many gourmet restaurants outside of the island. One of the simplest and most enchanting dessert beverages with which I have come into contact of late is the following invention of the Down Under Restaurant in Fort Lauderdale, Florida.

1 jigger dark or light Jamaica rum

1 scoop buttered pecan ice cream

cracked ice

Add rum, ice cream, and a handful of cracked ice to container of your electric blender. Whirl until blended but not smooth. Turn into a chilled pewter mug or cocktail glass and serve at once.

caribbean rum fruit ice
serves 6 to 8

Here we have a rum ice, simply made which uses the genuine article, Jamaica rum along with many other tropical ingredients.

2 tablespoons dark, or 3 tablespoons light Jamaica rum

4 ripe bananas, mashed

8 tablespoons canned pineapple juice

6 tablespoons fresh orange juice

2 tablespoons fresh lime juice

2 tablespoons granulated sugar

¼ teaspoon salt

½ pint heavy cream, whipped

¼ cup coarsely-chopped toasted cashews

In a large bowl, thoroughly combine the mashed bananas, juices, Jamaica rum, sugar, and salt. Gently fold in the heavy whipped cream. Place in freezing tray of refrigerator, and freeze until firm. Remove to a bowl, and beat, with rotary beater or wire whisk, until light and fluffy. Fold in the roasted cashews, return to the freezer tray, and re-freeze until just set. This usually takes about an hour.

index

The word *rum* has been deleted from entries wherever possible to conserve space.